D1238337

Computer Monographs

GENERAL EDITOR: Stanley Gill, M.A., Ph.D., Chairman, Software Sciences Holdings Ltd, London

ASSOCIATE EDITOR: J. J. Florentin, Ph.D., Imperial College, London

Introduction to Operating Systems

Introduction to Operating Systems

A. J. T. Colin

Professor of Computer Science
University of Strathclyde

Macdonald · London and
American Elsevier Inc. · New York

© A. J. T. Colin 1971

Sole distributors for the British Isles and Commonwealth
Macdonald & Co. (Publishers) Ltd.
49–50 Poland Street, London W.1

Sole distributors for the United States and Dependencies
American Elsevier Publishing Company, Inc.
52 Vanderbilt Avenue, New York, N.Y. 10017

All remaining areas
Elsevier Publishing Company
P.O. Box 211, Jan van Galenstraat 335, Amsterdam, The Netherlands

Macdonald SBN 356 03868 8
American Elsevier ISBN 0 444 19589 0
Library of Congress Catalog Card No. 78 165347

Made and printed in Great Britain by
Hazell Watson & Viney Ltd., Aylesbury, Bucks.

Contents

Preface

This book has been developed from notes written for a series of lectures on Operating Systems, given to students on a first degree course in Computer Science.

The book is not 'elementary' in the sense that it can be read profitably by someone with little or no computer knowledge. To understand it fully the reader should preferably be familiar with programming at machine code and higher levels, have some knowledge of logic design, and be acquainted with the user interface presented by at least one modern operating system.

Ideally, a course covering operating systems at the introductory level should take about 30–40 lectures. Of this time about half would be spent in actually presenting the material in the book; a third in illustrating it by discussing the ways in which the various concepts are implemented on a system familiar to the students; and a sixth in a detailed discussion of how to set up interacting processes in a small machine to which the students have direct access.

The course should be supported by practical work; among possible projects are the simulation of paging, setting up of interacting processes in a small machine, the design of a simple batch monitor, and the construction of editing programs of various sorts.

I would like to offer my thanks to numerous people for helping me write the book. To Professor Higman and my other colleagues at Lancaster University for suggesting some of the topics and for commenting on their presentation; to Miss J. White and Miss D. Daniels for typing and re-typing the manuscript; to members of my family for encouraging me, and lastly to my students, who not only made numerous constructive criticisms, but even provided me with some of the quotations at the head of the chapters.

Andrew Colin

1 Introduction

Question – '*What is an elephant?*'
Answer – '*A mouse with an Operating System*'.
> Folk saying.

The first programmable computers gave rise to a sudden increase in the complexity and scale of calculation made possible for mathematicians and engineers. For the first few years all that seemed to matter was that calculations which had been considered impossible for practical reasons could now be carried out by any scientist with access to the right equipment; little attention was paid to the actual amount of work needed to obtain the results, their reliability and the cost of obtaining them.

Initially, the extremely wide range of possible computer applications was not fully appreciated. The new machines were seen as ideal for calculating tables of different kinds, and it was seriously suggested that one computer would be sufficient for the needs of a whole country. It was not long, however, before scientists and businessmen began to see the potential importance of computers in their own fields, and the use of computers began to grow rapidly, This growth produced a subtle change in attitudes. At first programs had been written mainly by the same people who had designed and built the computers, or by their close associates. Program writing was considered an end in itself. The new users were far less interested in the mechanics of calculation; typically they wanted fast reliable results, for a minimum of preparatory work and at a cost which they could afford.

The needs of the new users, which are perhaps intuitively obvious to all (except computer manufacturers, who were slow to see them) can be stated formally:

(1) The design, coding and execution of algorithms must be made as easy as possible. This implies

    (a) the need for suitable languages to express the algorithms,

    (b) the need for special mechanisms to modify test and validate purported algorithms,

    (c) the need for the simplification of certain common procedures such as the calculation of elementary functions or the control of peripheral devices.

1

(2) The overall system must be reliable. This can be understood in two ways:

    (a) once a program has been satisfactorily developed, it must be possible to place a high degree of faith in the results it produces;

    (b) the service must be regularly available, not subject to unforeseen delays or gaps. There should be no 'catastrophes' which damage or destroy information which cannot be immediately replaced.

(3) The resources used by any program must be controlled. This again can be interpreted in two ways:

    (a) Any individual program must not be allowed to exceed limits of time, space or output which are decided by the user.

    (b) The distribution of the system's resources among all its users must be in accordance with a policy laid down by the computer management. In a system where demand is controlled by charging, each user (and also the management) should be kept well up to date on the value of resources he has consumed; where demand is controlled by rationing, no user should be permitted to exceed his agreed allowance.

(4) The system as a whole must give 'good value for money'. This implies that all its components must be as fully utilised as possible, and if several operations can be overlapped in time, so much the better.

These four requirements apply to every general-purpose computing system. Individual systems differ in various ways, chiefly with respect to the range of problem oriented languages provided, and the method of access available to the users, that is direct interaction with programs, or a batch processing service. Frequently there are special requirements such as the need to service remote terminals, or to look after special devices which must receive control signals within a critical time of making requests for them.

The methods of satisfying these demands have always been based on a mixture of hardware and software. Apart from problem-oriented languages, which have always been software-based, the trend at first was to design and construct hardware devices of increasingly great complexity. This led to a rash of expensive and relatively unreliable equipment for code conversion, automatic checking of blocks of transmitted data and similar tasks. Eventually it was realised that general-purpose processors driven by the appropriate programs could do all these jobs much more flexibly and reliably, and the cost of such processing is so low that now the trend has reversed. Most of the needs of a computing installation (other than the provision of raw computing power) are filled by specially designed software used in conjunction with a few simple hardware devices. It is this software, which is interposed between the user of the system and the basic hardware, which is called the 'operating system'.

The first generation of computers had a structure in which all components, including the basic peripherals, were controlled by a single unit. Overlapping of operations by different peripherals was permitted, but if a command was sent to a device which was still processing the previous command the entire system was halted until that command was complete. This meant that the speed of the whole machine was limited to that of the slowest component in use at any moment. Naturally, this state of affairs led to extremely low utilisations of many parts of the system. To give an example, the 'duty cycle' of the control unit of a typical first-generation machine when copying paper tape was less than 1 per cent.

The operating systems built for this kind of computer were intended mainly to reduce the delays to human operation by running whole sequences, or 'batches' of jobs automatically without human intervention. Although these systems are primitive when compared to modern operating systems, they can be used for peripheral control and to provide filing facilities. We discuss batch monitors, as they are called, more fully in Chapter 2.

A fundamental advance in computer design was made with the introduction of the 'interrupt'. This concept was first used in some computers built in the late 1950s. In a machine fitted with this facility, each peripheral device can be started by the central control unit, but continues to work autonomously. When it finishes its job, or needs attention for some other reason, it sends an 'interrupt', which usually stops the central processor from whatever it is doing, and makes it give its attention to the cause of the interrupt. Clearly, this system makes it possible to arrange for wide-scale overlapping of operations, at the cost of considerable complexity in software. All modern operating systems are based on machines with an interrupt facility; indeed, this is one of the 'simple hardware devices' we mentioned previously.

2 Batch Monitors

Batch monitors are primitive operating systems usually built to run on computers without interrupt facilities. Their prime purpose is to run whole sequences of jobs without human intervention, thus saving time which would be lost waiting for operators to respond to requests or initiate new jobs.

Batch monitors are chiefly useful in situations where the computing load consists of many short, simple jobs. In their basic form they merely automate the job cycle shown in Fig. 2.1:

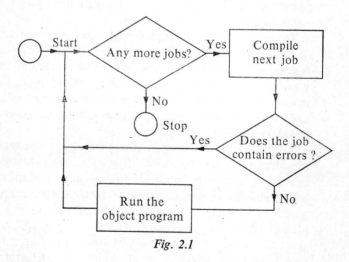

Fig. 2.1

It is necessary for the batch monitor to have control over the compiler and over the object program. This is achieved by writing the compiler in the form of a subroutine which is *called* by the monitor program. Similarly, the object program produced by the compiler is also cast in 'subroutine' form.

4

The typical core store layout in a system which uses a batch monitor is shown in Fig. 2.2. It will be seen that a substantial portion of the store is permanently assigned to the monitor, and only the remainder is usable by a compiler or object program.

Work is normally presented to a batch monitor as a 'job stream' on cards or paper tape. Each individual job is preceded by a 'job description' of one or more records, which indicates the identity of the

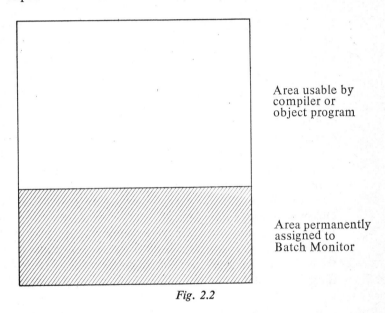

Area usable by compiler or object program

Area permanently assigned to Batch Monitor

Fig. 2.2

job and other necessary information, such as the compiler wanted (if the system provides a choice) or a request for a post-mortem dump when the job finally ends. The job itself includes a program and usually some data, and is followed by a special 'terminator' record with some distinctive format, such as '+ +' or '- - - -'. This record plays an essential role in the system; it allows the batch monitor to align itself with the beginning of the next job if the previous one happened to end in some abnormal way, without having used all its input. Generally, the terminating record of the last job is followed by a 'batch ender', a record with another distinctive format.

Ideally, all that the operator has to do when running a computer under batch monitor control is to ensure that all the jobs are properly

5

batched, load them into the appropriate input device, and start the computer. Unfortunately, the batch monitor has a number of fundamental drawbacks which mean that its operation is hardly ever as smooth as our description might suggest. The reason is that the monitor has no more control over the program it is running than any other program has over one of its subroutines. If the object program attempts to obey an illegal order, the whole system stops; if it gets stuck in a loop, it drags the system with it; and finally, there is nothing to prevent an erroneous object program from over-writing part of the monitor, thus producing a fault which may not become apparent until several jobs later. Illegal orders and monitor corruption can be avoided if the only access to the system is through a high-level language and a carefully written compiler which generates self-checking code, but indefinite looping can occur under almost any conditions. In practice, operator intervention to stop indefinite looping and to correct 'crashes' is needed rather often (typically once every 10 or 12 jobs) and in a fair proportion of cases the system is corrupted and must be restarted completely.

In addition to these fundamental drawbacks, batch monitors impose certain restrictions on programs run under their control. Object programs are specifically banned from writing anything into the area of the store occupied by the monitor, and direct interaction with the user, although possible, is discouraged because it holds up the entire system. The choice of languages tends to be restricted to those supplied by the manufacturer because each compiler and assembler has to be written as an integral part of the system.

In spite of these difficulties batch monitors have achieved widespread use, particularly in universities and schools where the load consists largely of many small jobs.

Once the basic principle of the batch monitor had been invented it became clear that various additional facilities could be incorporated. Two of the most important of these are the automatic control of peripherals, and the provision of a filing system.

In a computer without an operating system, the correct control of peripherals can be quite complicated. Each peripheral device may have a series of 'flags' or single-bit registers which are accessible to the program and indicate the state of the peripheral or the success or failure of the last transfer. Even the 'elementary' operation of, say, punching a card requires the following program:

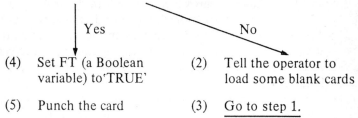

(1) Test the card punch flag which indicates whether there are any cards in the input hopper

      Yes   No

(4) Set FT (a Boolean variable) to 'TRUE'   (2) Tell the operator to load some blank cards

(5) Punch the card   (3) Go to step 1.

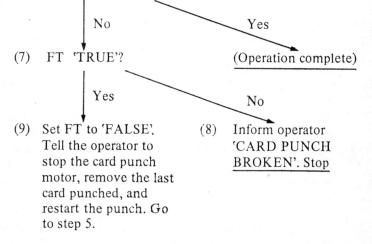

(6) Test the card punch flag which indicates whether the last card was punched correctly

      No   Yes

(7) FT 'TRUE'?   (Operation complete)

      Yes   No

(9) Set FT to 'FALSE'. Tell the operator to stop the card punch motor, remove the last card punched, and restart the punch. Go to step 5.   (8) Inform operator 'CARD PUNCH BROKEN'. Stop

In this procedure, the commands to the operator may be typed on a special console, or they may be coded as combinations of lights which appear on a panel.

If a batch monitor is used, driving procedures for all the peripheral devices can be written into it once and for all, and there will be no need to write them into every single program which is run on the machine. Object programs no longer refer to the peripherals directly, but can call the driving procdeures in the monitor as subroutines. This saves both space and programming time, as well as ensuring that instructions to the operators are always in one standard format.

A filing system can be provided by a batch monitor if the machine has an adequate backing store. There can be a library of subroutines and complete programs which can be 'called', or incorporated into any job if they are mentioned, by name, in the appropriate format. The monitor must of course provide a method of updating the library when necessary; if the backing store is big enough, this facility can be used to store individual users' programs as well as the standard library.

There is, of course, a great deal more to be said about filing systems, but this will be left over until a later chapter.

Although the introduction of batch monitors resulted in a worthwhile increase in the amount of work which could be put through a computer, it was still the case that the speed of the whole system was no greater than that of the slowest component. In many installations, expensive central processors were almost totally idle for much of the time waiting for slow peripheral devices. An excellent solution to this problem was found in the technique of 'off-lining', first used by Purdue University in their 'PUFFTS' operating system.

Here, the overall system consisted of a fast 'main' computer (an IBM 7090) and one, or more, small slow machines (IBM 1401). The main computer did not control any slow peripherals, but depended entirely on magnetic tape for input and output. Each input magnetic tape was prepared by the 1401 by reading and copying a batch of jobs from punched cards; similarly, each output tape from the main machine was eventually processed by the 1401, which reproduced its contents on a line printer. The system was highly efficient because the main machine was no longer held up by input and output (the transfer rates for magnetic tape being very much higher than those for punched cards or line printers). Although the 1401 was limited to slow peripheral speeds, it was such a cheap machine that this did not lead to the waste of expensive computing power.

In spite of the operational problems involved in transferring magnetic tapes back and forth between two machines, the system is said, in some cases, to have improved the throughput on the IBM 7090 by a factor of five. It was among the most widely used batch monitors for machines of an early pattern.

Machines without interrupt facilities are now obsolete, and simple batch monitors of the type we have described in this chapter have begun to fall into disuse. There are, however, numerous examples of 'pseudo batch monitors' superimposed on operating systems of a more modern pattern. This is possible, because most full operating systems present the user with a 'virtual computer', which is apparently similar to a complete computer of an earlier generation. It is desirable because present-day systems are designed to deal with very complicated situations, and can be grossly inefficient when handling very simple jobs.

3 Programs and Processes

All computer users are familiar with the idea of a 'program'. Unfortunately, this notion is not powerful enough to describe the software needed to drive a modern operating system; but nevertheless it includes several important concepts which, if isolated, will help to understand the way in which the operating system is constructed.

When a program is run, we can distinguish three separate entities:
(1) The set of instructions, or *procedure*, which specifies the program.
(2) The *processor*, or agent which executes the procedure.
(3) The *environment*, which is that part of the world which the processor can directly sense or alter.

We regard the program as proceeding by a sequence of steps in time. For our purposes here, we can treat the steps as elementary, so that we are not concerned with the states of parts of the machine during the actual execution of any step. This means that our 'environment' must include any part of the machine or its surroundings which can be sensed or altered by program; it need not involve such components as memory address registers or buffers within the arithmetic unit. The environment *does* include accumulators and the control register of the computer, since these can be both altered and sensed by program.

The essential properties of a *program* are these:
(1) The operations specified by the procedure take place in a strictly sequential order, each single step being effectively completed before the next one is started. (By definition, we exclude from the category of 'program' any process which involves overlapped operations, except where the overlaps are organised by hardware fitted with interlocks so that the procedure need not be aware of them.)
(2) The environment is completely under the control of the program, and does not change in any way except as a result of steps taken by the program. Since the sequence of steps is determined by the con-

10

trol register, which is itself part of the environment, it follows that the order of operations is completely determined by the program itself. (Note – we do *not* say 'determined in advance'.)

(3) Except in so far as the results of a program are required within a reasonable time, the actual time taken for any operation is not relevant to the running of a program. Furthermore, it does not matter if there is a temporal gap in between any pair of steps. Lastly, it is by no means essential for the identity of the processor to remain constant for the whole execution of the program; it would be entirely feasible to change processors at any time, provided that the change did not alter the environment of the program.

The definition we have given of a 'program' implies that it is a 'closed system'. Once started, it cannot be subjected to external interference but will run, independently of happenings outside its own environment, until it halts of its own volition.

Most 'ordinary' programs (particularly those written in high level languages) are good approximations to the ideal we have specified. The difference is usually trivial, and involves access to a real-time clock or a set of switches which can be set by the operator. One very important aspect of such 'ordinary' programs is that they are repeatable (unless they actually refer to a real-time clock or set of switches) and it is therefore relatively easy to detect and correct errors.

Why are 'programs' (in the above sense) unsuitable for driving operating systems? There seem to be two main reasons:

(a) The operating system is supposed to use all the components of the computer efficiently. This implies that the operation of the various components must be overlapped.

(b) The system must provide a specified 'response time' to requests made of it. This varies from a few seconds in the case of conversational use to a few milliseconds for data logging or process control. Since the time of these demands is both unpredictable and uncontrollable by the system, it cannot be said that the order of operations is determined solely by the system itself.

At this point it is worth noting that if neither of these two reasons apply, then 'programs' can make perfectly adequate operating systems. Most batch monitors of early machines are indeed 'programs' which satisfy our definition. The same is true of those dedicated computers which control numerous devices by 'polling' or interrogating each device in turn to see whether it needs attention.

11

The first attempts to construct software which could handle over-lapped operations and deal promptly with unpredictable demands were made without any real theoretical insight. The results were adequate for simple systems, but when the environment was more complex, the software often took several years to reach an acceptable standard of efficiency and reliability. The chief difficulty which beset the writers was that the conditions which led to some error were unrepeatable, and the cause of the error, sometimes remote, would be almost impossible to track down.

These difficulties led to the introduction of the 'process' as one of the chief conceptual tools of the operating system designer.

A process is in many ways similar to a single run of a program. It consists of a series of non-overlapped steps, each of which senses or alters the environment in some specified way. It is usually controlled by a procedure which is itself part of (that is stored in) the environment. A process can be safely interrupted between steps, and it is possible to change processors in mid execution.

The essential difference between a process and the execution of a program is that the process is not a closed system; it may communicate with other processes, either explicitly in ways which we shall explain later, or implicitly by altering or sensing part of its environment which is shared with other processes. Environment shared in this way is often called 'Global', whereas that which is private to the process is called 'Local'.

When introducing the ideas of programming, it is usual to explain matters by saying:

'Consider the central processor. First it does this instruction, then that one, then depending on the value of the data, it may jump to this one; and so on.' The explanation works because the central processor is seen to be following a sequence of steps which lead to some goal.

In a large computing system, numerous processes will be active simultaneously. Any attempt to understand the nature of the system by considering the activity of the central *processor* itself is bound to fail, because the processor will be sharing its resources among several different processes. On the other hand, if we consider the *process* to be the unit of activity, and do not pay too much attention to the processor which is effecting it, the working of the system becomes much easier to grasp.

As we have said above, a process is a *single execution* of a procedure. This means that each process has a temporal 'life'; there is a moment at which it is 'born', or initiated; and another when it 'dies', having completed its work. In general, processes are initiated by other processes; but there is one 'master process' from which the chain of initiation starts. This master process must be started manually, when the machine is first switched on.

At any moment during the life of a process, its progress can be described by its 'state'. Before the process is started, and again if the process should be interrupted for any reason, the variables which describe the state are usually assembled into a 'state vector', which is stored until the process is started (or restarted), and which contains sufficient information for the process to continue without being aware that it was interrupted. The state vector will include enough information for the complete construction or reconstruction of the local environment (which includes the address from which the next instruction is to be taken).

Explicit communication between processes takes place through a 'mechanism' which, although software, is not itself a process. At this point, we shall only describe its function, and we shall leave its operation to the next chapter.

Whenever a process wishes to communicate with another process, it issues an 'extracode', which has the appearance of a machine instruction, but has the effect of calling a routine in the communication mechanism. In general, an extracode is a single order which calls *any* routine in the operating system. One can have, for example, extracodes which compute mathematical functions or manipulate characters. All extracodes mentioned in this chapter, however, are connected with communication between processes.

The communication extracodes fall into two groups. The first group is concerned with initiating and terminating processes. When a process A wishes to initiate another process B, it first assembles a suitable initial state vector (which of course includes the starting address of the procedure governing process B). It then issues an extracode which passes the starting vector to the communication mechanism, in a way which is roughly analogous to the initiation of a subroutine. The mechanism, however, starts up the new process and lets it run *at the same time* as the one which initiated it.

The second extracode in this group makes the communication mechanism terminate a process, irrespective of its current state. A process can attempt to apply this extracode to itself, or to any other process to which it can refer; it may not succeed, because not all processes can be stopped in mid-operation.

The second group of extracodes is devoted to manipulating and testing special communication markers, called 'semaphores'. Any part of the global environment of a process can be designated a 'semaphore'. The three types of semaphore extracode are:

(a) Change the value of a given semaphore in a stated way (for example by adding 1).

(b) Suspend the process which issues this extracode until a specified relation involving a semaphore becomes true. If it is already true, then do not suspend.

(c) Test whether a certain condition involving a semaphore is true; if so then apply a stated operation to the semaphore and proceed to the next instruction; if not then jump to a given address.

This last extracode must be considered as one operation. It would not be sufficient to code it as two separate instructions – a test followed by an alteration – because the value of the semaphore might be altered in between another concurrent process.

The reason that semaphore must be altered by extracodes (rather than by direct instructions) is that any such alteration may have the side effect of restarting some suspended process!

The name 'semaphore' was chosen because of the close analogy which can be drawn between process control and railway signalling. To illustrate the point, consider the following layout (Fig. 3.1):

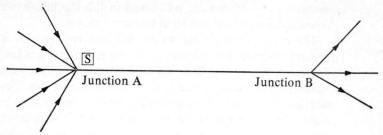

Fig. 3.1

Numerous trains arrive at junction A, and have to go down a single line to junction B, where they take their separate paths. The line joining A to B can take at most *n* trains at the same time. A large

14

signal (S) at A shows the number of trains, s, on the line at any moment. The procedure which each train driver has to follow is this:

    (1) Arrive at A.
  *(2) Stop (that is suspend all operations) until s is less than n.
  *(3) If s is *not* less than n, go to step 2. Otherwise add 1 to s.
    (4) Go down the line to B.
  *(5) On arrival at B, *subtract* 1 from s.
    (6) Go to destination.

The steps marked with an * are 'extracodes'. If a train arrives at A when there are fewer than n trains on the restricted line, there is no delay. If the line is full, each train will wait on its own branch line. When a train leaves the line at B, all the drivers waiting at A will be 're-activated', but only one will succeed in getting past the junction – presumably, the first one to notice the signal change. As the first driver to get past the signal will reset it to 'n', the others will see that $s \geqslant n$, and will go back to sleep at step 2.

As another example, we shall consider a 'data buffer'. Buffers can be used at any point where information arrives at a rate which may be different from that at which it leaves. A good example is a program which alternates bursts of extremely fast output to, say, a line printer, with long periods of calculation during which nothing is produced. If such a program is connected directly to the line printer, then its printing phases will be slowed down because the printer cannot keep up; during its calculating phases, the line printer will be idle.

The situation can be improved by inserting a buffer between the program and the printer. The buffer is an area of store which fills up rapidly when the program is generating output, and is then slowly emptied by the printer. The buffer acts as a reservoir, and the whole running of the program is speeded up because printing and calculation are now overlapped.

We suppose that the buffer consists of an area of store with capacity for n records, designated record (0) to record ($n - 1$). The area is assumed 'circular', so that record (0) is adjacent to record ($n - 1$).

The buffer has two associated pointers, p and q. p is the input pointer and indicates the record into which the next line may be written by the generating program. q is the output pointer, and marks the next record to be printed. The pointers are only advanced when the operations of input and output from the buffer are complete. The addition is done modulo n.

The buffer will be operated by two separate processes. One of them will be the run of the actual program which generates the lines to be printed, and the other will be solely responsible for printing out the buffer.

In this example, we are not at all concerned with the details of the actual calculation. All that matters is that the program generates lines at intervals. Normally, it will be able to write these lines straight into the buffer, but it must be prevented from doing so if the buffer is full. This will be the case whenever the values of p, the input pointer, and q, the output pointer, are equal.

The effective flow diagram for the program will be (Fig. 3.2.):

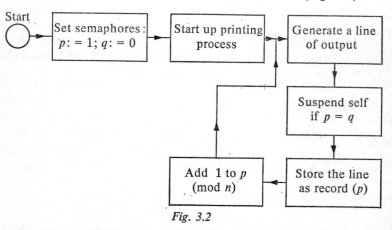

Fig. 3.2

The aim of the printing process will be to keep the line printer continuously busy unless the buffer is empty. This condition is indicated by the relationship $p = q + 1 \pmod{n}$. The flow chart for the printing process is (Fig. 3.3):

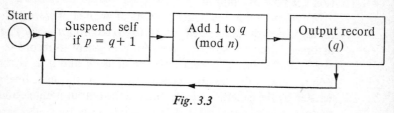

Fig. 3.3

For the sake of clarity, terminating arrangements are omitted in both flow charts.

16

It is convenient to regard a process as a method of altering the environment in some specified way. If this view is taken, it turns out that not all processes are controlled by sequences of instructions taken from the store. The main exception is the category of peripheral transfers, which move blocks of data of various sizes between different parts of the environment. This kind of process also signals its termination to the communication mechanism.

The reader is probably familiar with programs which refer to fixed parts of the computer, like 'register 100'. It is possible to write programs and procedures in such a way that the actual location of both global and local areas are not constant, but supplied at run time, as part of a 'state vector'. The simplest way of doing this is to supply a base 'address', which is added to all data store references at run time. A procedure which has this property is very useful in an operating system, because it can be used to drive several independent processes simultaneously. Thus, several different buffers of the type we have just described can be controlled by one single procedure. This kind of procedure is called 'pure'. Another essential property of a pure procedure is that it never alters itself (that is its own code) in any way.

In systems which have many simultaneous users great savings of store can be made by using pure procedures. The store of a large multi-access system need contain only one copy of each of its standard service programs to service the demands of dozens or hundreds of users, although, of course, each user must have his own process with its own data area.

4 How processes are controlled

In the previous chapter, we established that a process consists of a sequence of one or more simple steps, designed to change the environment in some specified way. A process can be interrupted in between any two steps, and can be restarted later without ill effect, provided that the local environment is completely restored to its state before the interruption.

At any moment, the computing system contains numerous processes. Some are 'suspended', because they have issued 'suspend-me' extracodes. Processes which are not suspended are called 'free'. It is worth noting that any process which has terminated is not a dead process; it simply does not exist, any more than an individual performance of a play after the curtain has come down.

In this chapter, we shall consider the design of a machine capable of executing concurrent processes. Our first approximation to this design will appear very unusual, and will in fact be totally uneconomic, but we shall perform successive iterations to arrive at a conventional layout without sacrificing any basic principles on the way.

Our initial design will have three types of component: environment, processors, and control. The environment will comprise everything which the computer can sense or change, including all types of store, the data in input peripherals, and even the blank cards or paper in the output peripherals.

The processors will include all devices which can effect a change in the environment, and will fall into two groups:

(a) 'central' processors, which are driven by stored instructions taken from somewhere in the environment, and

(b) 'peripherals', which operate according to fixed, built-in control sequences.

We note that by this definition, a device such as a tape punch must be considered a kind of *processor*, because it can change the environment by making holes in a strip of paper which was previously blank. It is also convenient to include (human) operators and other people in contact with the system in this category, although such 'processors' are exceptionally slow and unreliable by hardware standards.

Both types of processor have the property that once primed with appropriate data (such as the address of the first of a sequence of stored instructions, or that of an area of store whose contents are to be transferred), they can be started and left to run autonomously. It will be possible to have many processors running simultaneously, and we shall take for granted the fact that clashes in access to the store are resolved by a queuing system implemented in hardware. We also assume that there are enough processors of different types to service any new process as soon as it is created.

The third component of the machine is the control. In our first approximation, this will consist of a dedicated central processor, driven by a control procedure somewhere in the store. The control processor will have special lines of communication with all the other processors. It will be able to start them with any initial conditions, and will be informed whenever any processor ends the process it is running, or obeys a communication extracode. The control processor will keep records of all the processes currently in existence, and the reason for their suspension, if any. Normally, it will wait, doing nothing, until an event occurs. On being activated, the control will determine the cause of the activation, will make the appropriate adjustments to its table of processes, and, if possible, will restart the processor which produced the event. If the event was an extracode to create a new process, the control processor will start the new process too. We note that to work correctly, any central processor issuing a communication extracode must suspend itself until it is restarted by the control.

Unlike a processor running its own process, the control processor is not really in command of events. All the other processors run at their own speed, and may require attention at any time. It would not be feasible for the control processor to abandon the servicing of one processor if a service request was received from another, so any events which happen when the control is busy are placed in a queue. Whenever the control finishes serving any device, it always makes sure that this queue is empty before returning to the quiescent state.

At this stage, our system has the overall structure of Fig. 4.1.

We shall now start on our iterations. In the first instance, it is grossly uneconomic to provide so many processors that there is always one ready for every new process. We must make do with fewer and accept that processes will sometimes be held up just because no

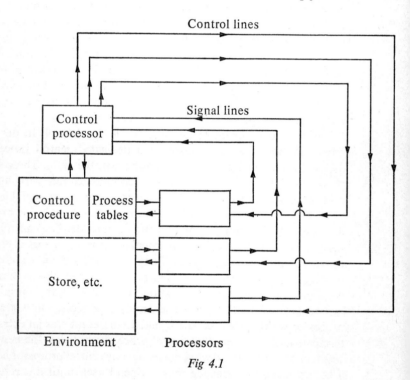

Fig 4.1

processor is available to move them forward. This immediately gives rise to an allocation problem, since every time that a processor is freed a decision must be made about which process to assign it to next. This choice is always taken by the control, using a 'scheduling algorithm', which we shall discuss in a later chapter.

In general, the control processor can make better allocation decisions if it can dispose not only of any processor which may be free, but of all the central processors in the system. To make this possible, it must be fitted with a mechanism to interrupt the other processors in such a way that what they are doing can be restarted later.

In the next iteration, we notice that most of the time, the control processor is doing nothing. We shall therefore dispense with it as a separate entity, and distribute its function among the other central processors in the system. This implies that each central processor will play two roles, and must be able to switch between two slightly different sets of properties. In the 'normal mode', it will be effecting a process, and will be liable to interruptions from the processor currently filling the control function (as we shall see in a moment, it may also be liable to interruptions from peripherals). In the 'control' mode, it will not be interrupted, and is given a measure of control over the other processors in the system.

In the 'control' mode, often called 'interrupt' mode, although a better name would be 'non-interrupt' mode, all the processors are driven by a single copy of the control procedure. It is possible for several processors to be in the control mode simultaneously, and great care must be taken to ensure that they do not interfere with one another in manipulating process state tables.

To activate the control program we set up the following system:
(1) Whenever a process running in a central processor issues a communication extracode, the same processor is switched into the control mode and takes appropriate action. This ensures that any process which gives such an extracode is automatically suspended.
(2) Whenever a peripheral process ends, the device signals its termination by sending an 'interrupt'. This is routed to one of the central processors, which is switched from normal into control mode and deals with the event appropriately. This will usually involve restarting the peripheral device which produced the interrupt as soon as possible. The routing of the interrupt can be made by a device like a uniselector; it merely examines the central processors sequentially until it finds one which is not in the control mode. If all the processors are in control mode, the interrupt is placed in a queue.

Whenever any processor ends its control function it re-allocates itself to some free process and switches itself back into normal mode. The process selected need not be the same as that which was interrupted.

An alternative system for a machine with several central processors is to steer all the interrupts to one processor only. This gives the advantage of simplicity, since only one of the processors need be able to work in two modes or have any control over the others. On the

21

other hand, it may take longer to service any given event, and is much more sensitive to breakdown than a system in which the control function is distributed. Lastly, we shall mention the special case of a system with only one central processor. The case is important, since it gives a picture of most existing systems.

To illustrate these ideas, we shall describe a one-processor system in a little more detail. This will not be an exact description of any existing machine, but will be a representative and simplified abstraction.

We shall suppose that the machine has core and disk stores, a card reader and a line printer. The configuration is as shown in Fig. 4.2.

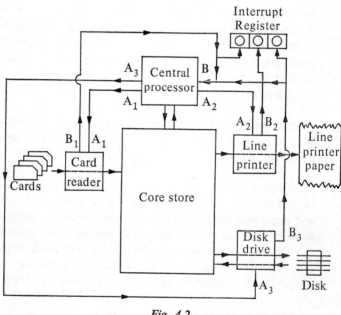

Fig. 4.2

Initially, we suppose that all the peripherals are quiescent, and that the central processor is running a process controlled by stored instructions. At some time, this process may issue an extracode asking for a peripheral process to be started up. The central processor will switch into the control mode, and will activate the appropriate peripheral down one of the lines marked A_1 to A_3. It will then reallocate

22

itself to the process it was running before. Soon another peripheral process may be initiated. Eventually one of the peripherals will finish its transfer, and signal the central processor by setting a bit in the 'interrupt register' (a special hardware register) and sending a signal along line B. This will interrupt the central processor and switch it into the control mode. The processor will immediately record enough information about the process which was interrupted for an eventual resumption, and will then examine the interrupt register to discover which peripheral caused the interrupt and deal with it appropriately. If another interrupt arrives while the first one is being processed, a bit will be set in the interrupt register, but the processing of the previous interrupt will not be disturbed.

Next, we shall give some more detail about one possible form which the process tables may take. We shall assume that the machine is one which permits the use of pure procedures, so that any process driven by stored program has two important attributes:

(a) the address from which the next instruction is to be taken;
(b) the address of the data area, which is to be added to each data reference when the process is run.

In a peripheral process, the important parameters are the type of peripheral and the address (or addresses) of the data to be transferred. Furthermore, each process may be 'free', or suspended until a relation involving a semaphore is satisfied.

The basic record for each process will then consist of several distinct fields. Each record will be marked with the type of processor needed, and then the various other parameters will follow in some standard format. Each record will also have a status which will be 'free' or 'suspended until semaphore x satisfies condition y'.

Nearly all the activity of the control procedure can be expressed in terms of manipulating these records:

Event	Action
Extracode to initiate a new process.	The procedure constructs a new record and adds it to the list.
Extracode to terminate a procedure, or interrupt from a peripheral device to signify completion of operation.	The procedure finds and removes the record from the list.

23

Event	*Action*
Extracode to suspend a process until a condition is satisfied.	The procedure first checks the given condition. If not satisfied, it locates the record of the process referred to, and marks it as suspended for the given reason.
Extracode to change the value of a semaphore.	The processor makes the alteration, and then searches for all the records suspended waiting for a condition involving this semaphore. If appropriate, it changes their status to 'free'.
After every event.	The procedure searches the list of records and chooses one with free status to activate next. It does this for each free processor, including (finally) the central processor itself.

If the control procedure had to perform all these operations on a set of records stored as an array, it would be very slow. To speed matters up, it is usual to use list processing techniques, and to chain the records together in various ways. There would certainly be a chain of records of free processes, and for each semaphore there would be a chain of associated suspended processes. Garbage collection problems would be avoided by carefully returning each record to a free space list as soon as it was no longer needed.

To finish this chapter, we shall mention the notorious 'deadly embrace'. This occurs whenever two processes interact in such a way that neither can advance until the other has completed some operation. As an example, consider the following:

Whenever a process wishes to write to a non-local area of store, it usually checks that a semaphore associated with the area of store shows that the area is 'free', and then immediately changes the value of the semaphore to marked the area as 'reserved'. When it has finished with the area, it resets the semaphore to 'free'. Now consider two processes, running concurrently. One of them attempts to reserve areas A, B in that order, whereas the other attempts to reserve

24

them in the order B, A. If both processes succeed in reserving one area each, it is evident that neither can move forward; they are in deadly embrace.

This situation can be avoided by careful programming. The whole question is discussed more fully in a later chapter.

5 Virtual Addressing

Consider the environment of a computer. Every part of it has its own identification; for example each register of core has its unique physical address, and every peripheral device has its number by which it is identified.

In a very simple computer, the addresses produced by any program (after modification or indirection, if any) are exactly those used to make reference to the environment. When the program refers to register '7740', for example, the programmer can be sure that the physical cores are those which the installation engineer would also know as part of word '7740', and if such a reference produces an incorrect result, the programmer can tell the engineer exactly where the fault lies.

In other computers, the state of affairs is more complex. The program is separated from the environment by an 'address translation mechanism', and each address generated by the program is transformed by this mechanism before being used to access or record data in the environment. The address translation mechanism is not under the direct control of the program, and may not usually be by-passed except by procedures which run in the control mode. The result is that the programmer may not know where in the environment his program or data are actually stored, or which physical peripheral device he is using.

If the programmer ignores the existence of the address translating mechanism (as indeed, under most circumstances, he must do) he is aware of a series of registers and peripheral devices which comprise a 'virtual environment'. In nearly all cases, the virtual environment is a rearranged subset of the real environment. Every virtual element has a corresponding real element, but the converse is not usually true.

Environments, both true and virtual, may be divided into two regions – core store and peripherals. In this chapter and the next, we shall consider only the first of these regions; we shall discuss methods of using 'virtual peripherals' later. An address which is used to refer to a register in a virtual core store is called a 'virtual address', and the set of all virtual addresses in any situation is called a 'virtual address space'.

At this stage, we shall explain why virtual addressing is desirable. There are three main reasons:

(1) *Uniformity of address space*   Consider a system in which there are numerous concurrent processes. Each process will have its own local environment, and certain areas of the total environment will be shared among processes in some complex way. In a machine without a virtual addressing system, the writer of each procedure would have to know, in advance, exactly which part of the store his procedure was going to refer to. This requirement would not be too difficult for procedures which form part of the operating system, but it would be burdensome to those users of the computer who write their own programs. If the system were designed to run only one program at a time (like a batch monitor) it would still be possible to specify that all users' programs must run within a stated area of core store (for example registers 20000 to 77777). If, on the other hand, the system were intended to run more than one user's program simultaneously in a reasonably flexible manner, then the requirement (of writing the program to work in a predetermined part of the real store) would be impossible to fulfil, because the exact position of any user's program would depend on what other programs were being run at the same time, and would be unpredictable when the program was being written.

This difficulty can be removed by a virtual addressing system which allows every process (including users' programs) to be written into a uniform virtual store starting at register 0 and extending as far as necessary. (This idea will have to be modified slightly for processes controlled by pure procedures; we explain later.) The programmer does not need to know where his process is actually going to run, for each reference to his virtual store is translated to a real reference at run time by the address translation mechanism. (It must be emphasised that this translation has nothing to do with any substitution of symbolic addresses when a program is assembled prior to running).

(2) *Store protection*   Any system designed to run programs written by computer users must be protected against programming errors.

An incorrect process must not be allowed to corrupt any part of the environment which is the province of any other process, or to spoil the tables used by the control procedure. It is particularly important that users' programs in a multi-programming system be protected against one another; otherwise a program which has been checked out and is known to be correct may start producing wrong results because some quite different program has interfered with it. No programmer can ever be trusted to write error-free programs, so the protection must be enforced by the operating system itself.

Virtual addressing can be used for this purpose, too. Every store reference produced by a process can be checked to ensure that it lies within the virtual address space assigned to that process; if it does not, the process can be stopped, and the reference suppressed before it does any damage.

(3) *Store reorganisation* It often happens that the real store of a system has a layout which is not very convenient for programming. Typically, a system might have a smallish core store backed up by a drum or disk, whereas programmers find it convenient to write for a machine which has a very large 'one-level' store in which each element is equally accessible. Again, virtual addressing can be used to provide a large one-level virtual store, and to map it on to a real store of inferior characteristics. Store reorganisation is commonly implemented by 'paging', which is discussed in the next chapter. If this reorganisation is not needed, then the other two advantages of virtual addressing can be implemented by a system based on 'relocation registers'.

Suppose that we wish to provide a contiguous area of virtual store, starting at some constant address (usually 0). This will be mapped on to an equal area of real storage in such a way that virtual address k corresponds to real address $(k + b)$, where b is constant. The translation is done with the aid of a pair of relocation registers, called 'datum' and 'limit', respectively. The datum register contains the number b, and the limit register the number $(b + s)$, where s is the number of registers in the virtual address space. Whenever the process using this virtual store produces an address, the address is checked and translated from its virtual into the corresponding real form by the following mechanism (which is of course implemented in hardware) (Fig. 5.1):

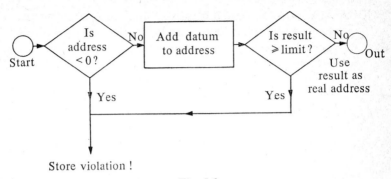

Fig. 5.1

Any reference within the virtual address space is converted to a real address by the addition of the datum value. The virtual address mechanism catches any 'reference' outside the space (whether above or below) and then generally activates the control procedure by producing a 'store violation interrupt'. The control mechanism takes appropriate action, usually terminating the process which produced the violation and activating a standard 'post-mortem' process with appropriate parameters.

A simple process (that is one which is not driven by a re-entrant procedure) only needs one contiguous area of store in which to work. The area can be chosen to include the driving procedure and all its local and global environment. Some machines are equipped to run processes of this kind, and have just one pair of relocation registers. Re-entrant processes, on the other hand, need at least two contiguous areas, one for the procedure and one for the data. Machines designed for handling re-entrant code are always equipped with at least two pairs of relocation registers, and sometimes more, for each processor in the system. The processor will direct 'program' references, taken from the control register, to one pair of relocation registers, and 'data' references to the other. This makes it impossible for a process to over-write the procedure which controls it, provided only that the procedure and data areas do not overlap.

When the control decides to reallocate a central processor to a new process, one of the things it must do is to set up new values in the relocation registers. These values for any given process are naturally part of its state vector.

29

As a special case, it is worth noting that if the control is switched between two processes controlled by the same procedure, then only one pair of relocation registers – that which refers to the data area – need be changed.

To make all these changes possible, and for certain other tasks (such as setting up new processes) certain procedures must be allowed access to the whole system. This is easily achieved by setting 0 in the datum register and some very large number in the limit register. The relocation registers themselves can be treated as peripheral devices, and can normally be altered only by a processor in control mode.

Lastly, the mechanism as we have described it is usually modified when built into practical systems. The addition and comparison of two numbers, each one as long as a store address, would take long enough to slow down the whole address transformation mechanism substantially because of carry propagation time. It is therefore common to omit several of the low order digits from the relocation registers, giving them the effective value of 0. This means that the numbers in the relocation registers must be multiples of 2^n (where n is the number of digits omitted) and implies that the size of each contiguous area of store must be a whole number of 'blocks', where the block size is 2^n. The actual block size in the smaller ICL 1900 machines is 64 words (6 bits omitted) and in the DEC PDP/10, 1024 words (10 bits omitted). The time which each the virtual addressing mechanism adds to each store reference on these machines is about 0·1 microseconds.

On the 'Titan' (a pre-production model of the ATLAS II computer at Cambridge University) the timing problem is solved in a different way. The contents of the register is not added to the virtual address, but 'or-ed' with it. This avoids the possible propagation of carries, but places strict and rather complicated restrictions on the sizes and locations of the real areas which may be used for virtual addressing spaces.

6 Paging

Olivia – '. . . *Where lies your text?*'
Viola – '*In Orsino's bosom.*'
Olivia – '*In his bosom? In what chapter of his bosom?*'
                    Twelfth Night Act I Sc. v.

Certain computers – mainly large ones – are fitted with mechanisms for 'paging'. This method of virtual storage not only fills the aims of store protection and the provision of uniformity which can be provided by relocation registers, but also permits the reorganisation of the store in a way which makes for easy and efficient programming.

With a paging system, each process works in a very large, uniform, virtual store. This confers several immediate advantages:

(1) Programmers need no longer worry about 'overlays' of program.

(2) Unless a body of data is very large indeed, it can all be held in the virtual store, and does not need to be 'sectionalised' for easy storage on a backing medium.

(3) Dynamic structures can be easily implemented, since they can be allowed to grow almost indefinitely. One program can have many stacks queues and similar structures, and provided that each structure is rooted in a virtual address which is sufficiently far away from the roots of other structures, there is no danger of mutual interference. This aspect is particularly useful in compiler writing.

The virtual store in a paging system will be divided into a number of 'blocks', which have a fixed size which is always a power of 2. The programmer need not be aware of this division, since the first register in any one block is considered adjacent to the last one in the previous block.

The real machine on which paging is implemented usually includes a fast core store of moderate size (smaller than the virtual address space) and a much larger backing store on disk, drums, or slow mass core. The fast core is divided into 'pages' each of the same size as a block in the virtual store, and the backing store is similarly divided into 'sectors' of the same size.

Consider the user's virtual space. Over any short period of time, the blocks in the space can be divided into three categories:

(1) the 'active' blocks, which contain words which are currently being used for program or data;

(2) The 'quiescent' blocks, which contain program or data which is not being used at the moment;

(3) the 'imaginary' blocks, in which no word has been referred to even once in the whole run of the program so far.

The distinction between categories (1) and (2) is dynamic and rather blurred, since blocks will be continually changing status as the program proceeds. Blocks in category (3) are only common where the virtual address space is extremely large (like 10^6 words).

The virtual addressing mechanism has the task of mapping this virtual space on to a real environment. It is important that the active blocks be found within the core store, but the imaginary blocks need not be represented at all. The quiescent blocks may be kept either in the core, or on the backing medium whence they may be fetched when needed.

The first computer system to use paging was the Ferranti ATLAS which was designed at Manchester University in 1958. It is still, at the time of writing, one of the most successful paging machines in existence.

On the ATLAS, the virtual address space is almost 2^{20} (10^6) words long, and is divided into about 2000 blocks of 512 words each. The core store has a number of pages, also of 512 words. The actual number of pages differs at various installations, ranging from 32 to 96. The backing store is a drum with about 250 sectors, also of 512 words each.

Whenever the ATLAS is running a process which requires a virtual store, then some of the blocks of this process are placed in certain pages of the core. Other blocks are stored on the drum. In neither case is there any fixed relationship between the block numbers and the addresses of the page or sector where they are stored; the actual relationship is stored in a table which is maintained by the operating system. Even though a process may be active, other pages of the core store may contain parts of the operating system, tables, or blocks belonging to other processes. The same is true of the backing store.

The translation between the virtual and the actual addresses is done with the aid of 'page address registers'. One of these registers is attached to each page, and contains the number of the block current-ly occupying that page, together with three independent digits called a 'use bit', a 'write bit', and an 'active bit', respectively.

When the process submits a virtual address for translation, the address is first split into a 'block number' and a 'line number'. This is easily done because the block size is always a power of two. The block number is simultaneously compared with the contents of *all* the page address registers, and the only one to respond (if any) will be one which contains the same number and an 'active' bit set to 1. The page address register responds by producing the number of the page it is attached to, and this number is combined with the line number taken from the original virtual address, to make a real

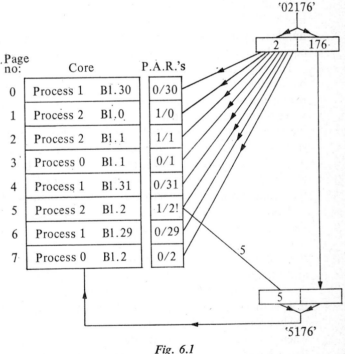

Fig. 6.1

address which can access the core store. The whole process takes about 0·1 microseconds, the same as the addition of a number from a relocation register. The process is illustrated in Fig. 6.1. Here, the core store is 8 pages long, and contains blocks of various processes as

33

shown. In the page address registers, we show the activity bit and the block number, but not the use or write bits. Process 2 is active (hence its activity bits are set to 1), and all the other processes are not active. In the example, the process generates the virtual address 02176 (octal). This is split into a line number (176) and a block number (2). The block number is transmitted to all the page address registers, and the only one to respond is the one attached to page 5, because it contains a 2 and its activity bit is 1. (Note that the page address register of page 7 does not respond, because the '2' it contains refers to a different process which is not currently active.) The output of the responding page address register is combined with the original line number to give a real address, 5176, in the core store.

It will sometimes happen that none of the pages contains a wanted block. If none of the page address registers responds to a block number, then the address translation mechanism generates a 'non-equivalence interrupt' and activates the control procedure.

The response of the control to a non-equivalence interrupt depends on whether the block mentioned has hitherto been imaginary or merely quiescent. In the former case, the system checks that the total space allowance requested by the program will not be exceeded by the creation of the new block, and then selects a page in the core store, fills it with zeros, and makes the appropriate correction to the page address registers, so that the block can now be referred to. In the latter case, the system uses its tables to locate the wanted block on the drum, brings it down to the core store, and adjusts the page address registers. In both instances, the system has to make room in the core store by selecting one of the existing pages, and 'banishing' it to the drum. Clearly, it is important that if possible the page selected should be one which will not be referred to immediately after; the methods of ensuring this are decsribed later in the chapter.

We can now explain the uses of the two other special bits in the page address registers. The 'write' bit is set to 0 whenever a block is newly brought into the core store from the drum. It is set to 1 only when a word in that page is altered by the program. This means that whenever any page is eventually banished from the core store, the write bit will only be 1 if the contents of the page have been changed; otherwise the page will still be an exact copy of a block already on the drum. It follows that the operation of writing the page from core to drum can be skipped if the write bit is 0.

The 'use' bit is used to collect statistics about the way in which the pages are used. The use bit of any page address register is switched to 1 if that page is referred to. At intervals (every 0·1 of a second) the use bits are scanned by a special routine which records their status and resets them to 0. This information is used to optimise the selection of pages for banishment.

When the central control program decides to switch the central processor from one process to another, all it needs to do is to alter the 'active' bits in the page address registers. It is, of course, quite common to switch processes whenever a non-equivalence interrupt occurs.

It can be seen that the two ancillary aims of virtual addressing are supported almost automatically. Every process lives in an identical virtual address space, and provided that the active bits are properly managed, no process can possibly interfere with any other.

Associative storage of the type needed to construct page address registers is fairly expensive, and several large computers (including the IBM 360/67 and certain models of the ICL 1906A) use a system which has fewer page address registers than there are pages in the core store.

Consider a virtual address space of n blocks. To implement it, such a system maintains a table of n consecutive words in the core store, each word signifying where the corresponding block is stored (core, drum or nowhere). There is a small number (8 or 16) of associative registers which contain the page numbers and corresponding block numbers of some of the pages in the core. Whenever a virtual reference to some block is made, the translation proceeds in three stages:

First, the virtual block number is compared simultaneously with the block numbers in all the associative registers. If one of them responds, it produces a page number which allows the real address to be formed. In most cases, the translation process stops here.

If none of the page address registers responds, the second stage is reached. The virtual block number is used as an index to refer to the block table in core. This takes one core cycle. If the result shows that the wanted block is in the core store, then the page number obtained from the block table can again be used to calculate the real address. If, on the other hand, the wanted block is found to be in the backing store, or to be absent, an interrupt is produced and the control procedure takes the appropriate steps, which constitute the third stage.

Naturally, this system works best if the contents of the associative registers correspond to the most commonly used pages. This can be achieved in various ways. One method is to update the associative registers every time that the block table has to be referred to. A new entry is made for the block which could not be found, and the oldest entry in the page address registers is discarded to make room, the registers thus being used in a cyclic manner.

Now, we come to consider methods of optimising the allocation of real store to the blocks of a virtual storage space. The aim is to minimise the number of transfers between core and backing store. This aim is implemented by calling upon a 'page turning strategy' which is used to select a page whenever one needs to be banished.

Page turning strategies have been studied intensively for about 10 years, and two general results are known. First, it appears that almost any reasonable automatic page selection system can do better than an 'overlay strategy' devised by a human programmer. This is to be expected, since the page selection strategy can work on the basis of observed facts, whereas the programmer has to make predictions about the way the system will behave. The second result is more surprising; apparently the most carefully designed strategies, which involve complicated selection mechanisms, are only marginally better than systems of extreme simplicity. In one somewhat limited experiment, three methods (all rather naïve) were compared.

The first method used cyclic banishment, so that in a store with n pages, the blocks to be banished on successive occasions were those in pages $0, 1, 2, \ldots n - 2, n - 1, \ldots$

The second method chose a page at random, each page being equally likely to be chosen.

The third method selected the page which had been referred to the smallest number of times since the last non-equivalence interrupt.

These three methods were simulated with different block sizes, with different numbers of pages, and with virtual address spaces of various sizes. The method of cyclic banishment was generally the worst, and the other two seemed roughly equal, but in no case did the difference (in terms of the number of transfers needed to complete a certain task) vary by more than 10 per cent.

The method used on ATLAS is to keep records of the usage of

each page for a number of consecutive time intervals of 0·1 second. The page turning algorithm first tries to select a page which has been unused for the longest time. If all the pages have been used in the most recent interval, then it chooses the page which has the most steeply descending rate of usage. The method is twelve years old but nothing substantially better is known.

It is of course possible that a page turning strategy will be invented which will be a real improvement on those currently in use; but the general ignorance on this subject is shown up by a recent paper, which reported that under certain conditions a paged process could be speeded up by *decreasing* the amount of real storage available to it. It is worth mentioning that the process was not a pathological one but one encountered in everyday running of the computer in question.

7 Peripherals (1) Control

In this chapter and the next two, we shall consider some of the characteristics of peripherals and the software needed to drive them.

As far as the operating system is concerned, each peripheral device is an autonomous processor for transferring information between various parts of the environment. The central control procedure can communicate with each peripheral either by sending it commands, or by interrogating its current state. The state at any moment can be represented by several binary digits, or 'flags', as follows:

Operable/Inoperable   If this flag is up, it indicates that the device is on and in working order; down, it means that the device is either switched off or stuck (due to, say, a lack of paper or a card wreck).

Busy/Free   This digit shows whether the device is currently busy on a transfer, or whether it is free to start a new transfer.

Right/Wrong   This flag is only meaningful on devices which check their own operation automatically, like card readers which sense every column twice. It indicates whether the last transfer to be made had a suspected (or known) error.

Naturally, these digits are not fully independent, since not every possible combination is meaningful.

Whenever a peripheral device is operable and free it can be started by an appropriate command. The type of command and the amount of information required vary according to the sort of device used. Some devices (such as disks or magnetic tape) operate in several modes, and must have the mode indicated in the command.

There are two basic ways in which peripherals can be connected to the central system. In some machines, each peripheral has its own 'communication register' which can be referenced by program in the same way as an ordinary store register. The control procedure can discover the state of the peripheral by 'reading out' the contents of

38

this register, and can send commands to the device by 'writing' suitable words into it.

In other computers, all the peripherals are connected to a single 'busbar'. Each device has its own unique numerical 'address', and every message which passes between any device and the central system is prefixed with address of that device. The busbar consists of a number of parallel channels; it appears as a single register to the control program, but this register is wide enough to contain both the command (or state information) and the address which must accompany it.

Although this difference is an important one from the architectural point of view, we shall not consider it further in this book. We shall merely assume that the central processor is capable of communicating with peripherals by the exchange of 'command' and 'information' words, which will of course have their own distinctive format and meaning for each peripheral type.

Another dichotomy of peripherals separates those which are 'autonomous' from those which are not. In a non-autonomous peripheral, all the information is transferred through the command or 'state' words, and the quantity transferred for each operation is small – usually one character. To illustrate the point, Fig. 7.1 shows a possible control word layout for an 8-bit character paper tape reader.

Go	Op/Inop	Busy/Free	Right/Wrong	8 information bits
11	10	9	8	7 – 0

Bit numbers

Fig. 7.1

We imagine that the tape reader is loaded with a paper tape which is stationary. If the control program reads the information word, it will discover from bit 10 that the reader is on and working, from bit 9 that is not actually moving the tape in between two characters, and from bit 8 that the parity of the character under the reading head is correct. The actual character itself is presented in bits 7–0. When the control has read and recorded the value of this character, it can start the tape reader moving on to the next character by sending a command word with '1' in bit 11. Thereafter, it must not attempt to read another character until bit 9 again says 'free'.

A non-autonomous punch might well have a similar control word format. To punch a single character, the control program would have to ensure that the punch was operable and free, and then write a control word which had bit 11 set to 1, and the digits of the character itself in bits 7 to 0.

Sometimes these detailed operations are disguised from the programmer by special micro-programmed instructions like 'branch on tape reader busy/free flag' or 'punch character in accumulator'. The basic principle, however, remains the same.

Autonomous devices work differently. Instead of transferring very small amounts of information through the control word, they communicate directly with the core store of the control system and move large quantities of information without interference from the control. The control channel is used only to initiate the transfer, or to report its completion (or failure). Fig. 7.2 illustrates the relationships between an autonomous device, the core store, and the control.

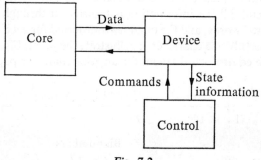

Fig. 7.2

Before it can begin a transfer an autonomous device must be supplied with at least one address – that of the core area concerned. If the amount of information can be variable, then this quantity must be made known, and if the device itself is addressable, then the address within the device must be given as well.

There are various ways of supplying this information. On machines which have a separate communication register for each device, the core address of the transfer is often placed in another special register which is also permanently allocated to the device. The same is true of the amount of information to be transferred. Other parameters, such as the track number on a drum, are transmitted by special commands, as discussed in the next chapter.

The operation of autonomous transfer devices places an extra load on the core store, since it has to supply the needs of the device (or even of several devices simultaneously) while still driving the central processors. The transfers are usually accomplished by 'cycle stealing', whereby, whenever a character or word is ready for transfer, an individual core cycle can be taken in between two successive instructions. If all peripherals are transferring simultaneously, the central processor can be slowed down substantially. If two or more devices make simultaneous demands on the core store, the conflict is resolved by a hardware priority mechanism.

Autonomous operation is optional for slow devices. With increasing speed, however, it rapidly becomes essential, because the central processor would not be fast enough to deal explicitly with each character or word.

Many devices have associated 'crisis times'. The crisis time is the maximum time which may elapse between the moment that a peripheral signals that some operation is ready, and the moment it receives the command to start the next operation. In some cases, there will be a catastrophic loss of information if the control system does not respond within the crisis time. This is true of all devices which are not autonomous but cannot be stopped within the space of one transfer; a non-autonomous card reader is a good example. Usually though, lack of response will mean nothing worse than a loss of speed. This can be very marked in peripherals which use rotating parts, because they are usually controlled by cams with photoelectrically sensed slits. Typically, an operation can only start as the cam passes through position $0°$, and the end of the operation is signalled nearly a whole revolution later – say at position $350°$. The command for the next operation must be given during the last $10°$ of the cycle, otherwise a whole revolution will be missed, and the device will only run at half speed.

As explained in Chapter 4, peripheral devices attract the attention of the central processor by producing interrupts. An interrupt occurs whenever a device changes from the 'busy' to the 'free' state, and activates the control procedure, unless all the central processors are already in control mode. In principle, the control procedure can discover which peripheral produced the interrupt by interrogating the states of all peripherals, one after the other; but since this would take far too long, in practice control is given a certain amount of help by special hardware arrangements. In most machines there is an interrupt register, which has a single bit for each device. The control procedure can read the contents of this register into an accumulator, and discover which bit has been set by obeying a very small number of instructions.

The procedure which deals directly with any peripheral device is called an 'interrupt routine'. Most interrupt routines attempt to get their subject devices back into operation as soon as possible.

Since the devices all operate concurrently, it is perfectly possible for more than one event, which would normally generate an interrupt to occur at the same time. It is also possible for a device to complete its operation at a time when no process can be interrupted to service it. If this happens, a bit will be set in the interrupt register, but no actual interrupt will occur. To cope with this eventuality, the control procedure always checks the interrupt register after obeying each interrupt routine; if any bit remains set, it is dealt with as if an interrupt had occurred.

If the interrupt register should contain more than one bit set, they will naturally be detected in a certain order. The device whose bit is noticed first is said to have the higher priority.

If the peripherals are to be correctly driven at their full speeds, certain relationships must be satisfied. Suppose that a system has n peripherals, numbered 1 to n in decreasing order of priority. Now let

A_k be the time interval between any two interrupts from device k, assuming it is driven at full speed;

B_k be the crisis time of device k;

C_k be the time needed to execute the interrupt routine for device k, plus essential overheads like analysing the interrupt register.

The first condition is that the central processor (assuming there is only one) must be fast enough to carry out all the necessary interrupt routines. For each device k, the number of interrupts per second will be $1/A_k$. The fraction of time spent servicing this device will be C_k/A_k. Since all the devices have to be serviced, the condition states:

$$\sum_{j=1}^{n} \frac{C_j}{A_j} \leqslant 1$$

For a system with q identical processors, this becomes

$$\sum_{j=1}^{n} \frac{C_j}{A_j} \leqslant q$$

The second condition specifies that in no case should the waiting time for any device exceed its crisis time. We shall only consider the case where there is one central processor. The worst case for any device k will happen if all the devices 1 to k inclusive demand attention simultaneously, just after the control processor has started on the longest interrupt routine, lasting C_{max} seconds.

Device k will have to wait for this routine to finish, and for all $k - 1$ devices of higher priority to be dealt with before it receives attention. The relation (which applies to each peripheral) is

$$C_{max} + \sum_{j=1}^{k} C_j < B_k \qquad \text{for } 1 \leqslant k \leqslant n$$

The machines we have been discussing so far have only two modes of running – normal and control. Some types of processor have several different levels of operation. Each peripheral device has its own characteristic level, and is only allowed to interrupt the central processor if it has a *higher* level than the one at which the processor is currently operating. This means that certain interrupt routines can themselves be interrupted. The resultant complexity is difficult to handle unless a disciplined approach is used, but great simplifications are possible if automatic stacking features are available for storing the current state of each level of interrupt. Multi-level interrupts are chiefly useful for machines in process control and real time applications, handling numerous devices with widely differing crisis times and interrupt routine lengths.

8 Peripherals (2)
The Operation of File Devices

File devices, such as magnetic tapes, disks, and magnetic cards are used to store very large quantities of information, some of it of considerable importance. Ideally, this information should be absolutely secure and incorruptible, but this desirable state of affairs is unattainable in practice. Even if it were feasible on technical grounds, there would still be the problem of physically protecting the media against fire and other accidental or deliberate damage. What can be done is to store the information in such a way that errors can be detected by the operating system and reported to the operator. With this facility, it is possible to design high-security systems based on the principle of storing the information several times over – preferably in different physical places. The organisation of such systems belongs to the realm of Systems Analysis; here, we shall confine ourselves to ways of detecting errors.

Let us start by considering magnetic tape. On the bulk of modern machines, the information is stored in variable-length 'blocks', separated by 'inter-block gaps'. The gaps are long enough for the tape transport mechanism to stop and start in between each block.

As far as the programmer is aware, the block to be recorded or read consists merely of a sequence of consecutive words in the store. On tape, the format is rather different, and includes additional checking information. The following description is representative of most actual systems:

When a block of information is recorded, the first item to go on to the tape is a special warning marker. Next, the words in the record are split up into 'characters' usually of 6 or 8 bits. The tape is divided into a number of parallel channels, one more than the number of bits in each character. Each character is recorded with an extra parity digit, all the bits being in parallel across the tape. The block is terminated by another warning character and a checking character in which each bit is a parity digit applied longitudinally to all the characters in the block. All the redundant information is generated, and later checked, by hardware.

The basic operations which any tape transport has to be able to do are these:

(a) write a block,
(b) read a block,
(c) backspace one block,
(d) rewind the tape.

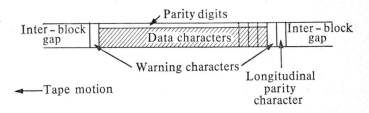

Structure of a data block on magnetic tape

Fig. 8.1

Some tape transports have a wider range of functions, and can read or write blocks backwards, and write or search for 'tape marks', which are a special kind of block detectable by hardware. As we shall see below, a very useful feature possessed by many transports is to be able to read at either of two amplifications – low and high.

Magnetic tape transports are activated by 'control words' in the same way as other, slower, peripherals. The transfers are invariably autonomous. The command word always includes several digits which specify the type of operation required.

During writing, each character in the block is checked for correct parity by being read back just after it has been written. During reading, the parity of each individual character is checked, and the longitudinal parity character is checked as well. This combination will detect nearly all errors except characters which consist wholly of zeros and are missing entirely, and these can be spotted by the operating system software, since the expected length of each block (in characters) is known.

An important characteristic of magnetic tape is that it is liable to deteriorate after repeated use. The layer of magnetic oxide wears

45

thin by rubbing against the reading and writing heads, and the level of the signal obtained when the tape is read drops until the record can no longer be deciphered at a given amplification. Another result of wear is the production of loose particles of oxide. These can get caught in the reading or writing heads of the transport and prevent it from working properly by lifting the tape away by a small fraction of an inch.

The interrupt routines which drive the tape decks are designed to minimise the effects of these difficulties. If a block is being written, and a failure is detected, the routine does not inform the operator immediately but backspaces the tape and attempts to write the block again. This happens up to 10 or 12 times, in the attempt to dislodge any offending particle of oxide or dust, which may be causing the trouble. In practice, the manoeuvre usually succeeds.

The interrupt routine which reads tape always starts by using low amplification. If an error is detected, it switches the deck to high amplification and attempts to read the block again, up to a dozen times. Only if this fails will the operator be informed.

The operating system keeps track of the number of 'repeats' needed on each tape deck, and whenever a tape is rewound the operator is given the total. This not only gives an indication of any tape deck which may be going out of adjustment, but also allows worn tapes to be removed from service before they cause a catastrophic loss of information.

With magnetic tapes, there is the serious difficulty of establishing and maintaining their identity. Unfortunately it is not enough to tell the human operators to attach a label to each tape; this is certainly essential, but is liable to an unacceptably high error rate both in writing the labels and in subsequently selecting tapes.

To overcome this problem, the operating system always writes or checks the first block on any tape. This block is called the 'header', and contains the tape's identification (typically a name and a generation number), the date on which the tape was last written to, and a 'retention period'. The operating system is thus able to check that no tape is used unless some program has specified it by name; if an operator loads the wrong tape, the system will tell him to unload it and put the right one on instead. Another check made by the operating system is that no tape is over-written until its retention period has expired. Still another security measure is afforded by the 'write permit ring'. This is a plastic ring which fits into the back of each spool of tape. When the spool is loaded, the ring presses against a micro-switch, which controls the circuits used for writing. If the ring is absent, the deck cannot write on the tape, irrespective of any commands it may receive from the central control. When the programmer specifies the name of a tape he requires, he also states whether the write permit ring is to be present, and the operating system checks that the tape is mounted as specified.

Properly used, all these safety precautions mean that undetected errors can be negligibly rare. However, in installations where there are many non-professional programmers, it is very common for tapes to be given absurdly high retention periods. To bring these tapes back into general use, a special program must be provided to over-ride the retention period and write a new header on to any tape. This program is sometimes misused, with somewhat painful results.

The management of disk and drum stores has several different features. On one hand, it is easier than the management of tape; there is no direct contact between the magnetic surface and the recording head, and there are therefore no problems of wear. Reading and writing failures are much more rare. On the other hand, a particular device may be used by several independent programs, and they must all be protected against one another.

The basic layout of data on a disk or drum also includes a quantity of checking information. The recording surface is divided into a large number of 'tracks'. Sometimes each track has its own read/write head, and sometimes there is only one head for each surface, which is moved from track to track by a stepping motor.

Each track stores information in 'blocks', which may be of fixed or variable length. The digits are recorded serially, and there is likely to be a parity digit after every character or word. The block is preceded by a warning sequence, and a number which gives the address of that block (as cartridge number, track number and block number within the track). The block is terminated by another warning sequence and a check sum formed from the contents of the block itself. The block is separated from the next one by a considerable gap, so as to allow the operating system to react in between blocks.

The controller of a disk or drum must have a rather large repertoire of operations. The controller is activated through a conventional control word, which has a format which gives both a 'function' and the value of the associated 'parameter'. Transfers to and from the core store are always autonomous.

The basic operations are:

(a) Stop the disk transport

(Used only if a cartridge has to be changed or after a detected error);

(b) Move the head to a specified track

(Only relevant if the heads are movable);

(c) Select a head.

(Applicable if there are several heads);

(d) Accept a block address

(Here the controller receives an address and stores it internally).

(e) Read a block of given address.

(Here the controller scans the leading addresses of blocks on the selected track until it finds one which matches the address it has stored internally. It then reads the following block, performing the necessary checks. If the device completes a whole revolution without the specified address being found, an error is signalled).

(f) Write a block of given address.

(This is exactly the same as (e) except that when the correct address has been read the block is *written*).

(g) Check a block of given address.

(Again this is the same as (e), except that the block is *compared* against the data in the core store, and an error is signalled if there is a discrepancy)

(h) Write addresses to a track.   (Here, the controller writes the specified address to the selected track. It may also write further sequential addresses at specified intervals. This mode is only used when a disk is being initialised).

(i) Read a whole track (including addresses).   (This mode is used only by engineers for investigating faults.)

The process of recording or reading a block from the disk or drum requires several sequential operations, thus:

(1) Move head to correct track (if heads are movable).
(2) Select track (if necessary).
(3) Set up a block address.
(4) Read a block.

or (4) Write a block.
(5) Check the block newly written.

It would appear that the address checking is not logically necessary, particularly if there is only one block per track. The reason for its inclusion is that it forms the only method of ensuring that the correct track has in fact been selected.

To the normal user, there are three levels at which these facilities can be supplied. At one extreme, the user can be allowed to operate the controller directly. This method gives great flexibility, but is obviously unsuitable if the same device is used by more than one independent program.

The second level gives each user 'virtual files', but still leaves their organisation to the individual user. Each device is divided into a number of regions (usually between 1 and 10). Each region has its own identifying name, and a special area on the device holds a directory containing the names and positions of the regions. The blocks within each region are given 'virtual addresses' starting at 0 (or sometimes 1). Adjacent blocks are given consecutive virtual addresses, but otherwise there is no connection between these addresses and the actual positions of the blocks on the device. The directory itself is accessible only to certain privileged programs.

With this system, the user is not permitted to operate the controller directly, but must leave all control to the operating system. He can 'open' a virtual file by specifying its name in a suitable extra-code.

The operating system searches the directory, and on locating the appropriate entry reads down the relevant constants and sets up a mechanism for translating virtual block addresses into their actual equivalents. When the file has been opened, the user can read or write blocks with given virtual addresses. Programs are protected from one another because the mechanism detects impermissible block numbers.

For protection of important data, files on a drum or disk are given a 'retention period', like magnetic tapes.

In a multiprogramming system, it is possible for several programs to access one file simultaneously. In one system, each file is given an 'integrity code', which indicates the extent to which multiple access is permitted.

Code 1: specifies that a file may be used by only one program at a time. This applies to 'work files'; for example a file into which a compiler is assembling an object program in some intermediate state.

Code 2: indicates that a file may be opened for reading only by any number of programs, *or* opened for writing by one program, but not both. This is suitable for library files, which should normally be accessible to all programs, but sometimes be closed for updating.

Code 3: specifies that a file may be written to by one program and simultaneously read by any number of programs. This is apposite to a data file for an information retrieval system, where the data base changes so rapidly that it must be continually updated; a good example is a file for holding current stock exchange prices.

Code 4: allows a file to be written to and read by any number of programs. The programs which do this will probably be part of a system of some kind, and they will have to observe certain disciplines; for example each program may be restricted to writing to one block only.

In a multiprogramming system, the operating system will receive numerous requests for transfers from different programs. If the device is a disk with movable heads, the system will not execute these demands in the same order as they arise but will attempt to minimise the head movements by sorting the demands into radial order.

The third level of sophistication in disk and drum usage is the automatic organisation of a complete filing system. This will be discussed in a later chapter.

9 Peripherals (3)
Their Appearance to the User

In previous chapters we explained the importance of allowing each user in a multi-programming system to write his program for a 'virtual store', and to use 'virtual files' for backing storage. The advantages conferred are, first, the provision of a uniform virtual machine (independent of the actual place where the program runs) and, second, protection against interference between independent programs. These arguments can be extended without modification to the provision of 'virtual peripherals'. There are even further benefits from such an extension. Peripheral devices usually include moving mechanical parts (unlike central processors) and spend a substantial fraction of their existence in an unserviceable state because they are broken or under maintenance; for example, in an installation with 8 or 10 tape decks, it is more common than not for at least one of them to be out of service. It is therefore a great advantage if a program is not rigidly associated with any particular physical device, but is free to use any device of the same type.

In all systems which permit multi-programming, the actual control of peripherals is exercised through interrupt routines by the operating system. Most multi-programming general-purpose computers have a built-in interlock which prevents any communication with peripherals unless the machine is in 'control' or 'interrupt' mode. Since a user's program cannot switch itself into control mode, it can only use the peripherals through the operating system.

For many purposes, peripheral devices are assigned to programs in 'real time'. The only 'virtual' aspect of such a peripheral is its identity; once a device has been assigned to one program, it remains in the sole possession of that program, and cannot be assigned to any other program until released by the first. This does not apply to inherently 'shareable' devices such as disks or drums.

In a system where this kind of peripheral assignment is used, the operating system keeps a table with an entry for each device on the machine. The entry indicates whether the device is

    (a) unserviceable,

or (b) serviceable but free,

or (c) currently assigned to some program.

In the latter case, the entry will show the identity of the program and also the 'virtual name' of the device to that program.

This table is searched and manipulated by the operating system for various causes. In one context, it can obey commands given by the human operators to mark given peripherals as unusable or to return them to the 'free' state after repairs. It can also accept instructions to assign particular devices to certain programs. This facility is useful if one device out of several similar ones has some temporary and unique property, like being loaded with specially pre-printed stationery.

In another context, it can carry out extracodes given by user's programs. For example, a program can issue an extracode which means: 'I want to use a card reader as my device number n' (where n is a parameter of the extracode). On being activated by such an extracode, the operating system will search the table for a free card reader. If it finds one, it will mark it appropriately. In any case, it will inform the program whether it has succeeded in getting the device or not.

Devices can be freed in two ways. Whenever a user's program is deleted from the machine, all its peripherals are released automatically. Alternatively, a user's program, which otherwise continues to be active, can give an extracode with the meaning: 'I have finished with my device number n.'

Once a program has reserved a device, it may use it by issuing transfer extracodes. These always refer to the device by its *virtual* name or number, and this is translated into an actual identity by the operating system, which uses the peripheral allocation table. A straight search down the table is usually avoided by using some sort of chaining to link entries for devices used by each program, or possibly an index to the various entries.

The easiest way to operate peripherals (from the programmer's point of view) would be for the system to suspend any program which issued a transfer extracode until that extracode had been carried out. For example, it would be convenient if the program could give an extracode to read a card to a given location, and then, in the next instruction, assume that the data on the card was already in that location. Unfortunately, this approach would not allow the program to operate more than one peripheral at a time, and might also lead to difficulties in meeting the crisis time requirements of any device. A compromise is therefore adopted; when the program issues a transfer extracode it is allowed to continue without suspension unless the device in question is still engaged on the previous transfer; and if the program is stopped for this reason, it is restarted as soon as the previous transfer is complete. This provision makes it possible for the user's program to use double-buffering and to operate many peripherals at the same time.

At this point, we shall give a brief explanation of the principles of double-buffering. The reader who is already familiar with this idea may skip to the next section.

Suppose that a program is reading cards on a reader that takes 100 milliseconds per card. The program has to process each card, taking 50 milliseconds to do so. If the program had to alternate between waiting for the next card and processing it, there being no overlap, the total time would be 150 milliseconds per card.

In a double-buffered system, the user's program would contain two data areas, each one sufficient for one card. The flow chart program would be (Fig. 9.1):

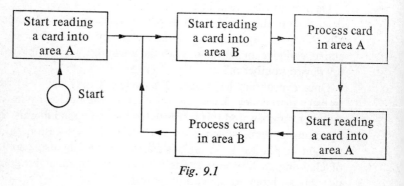

Fig. 9.1

The program begins by initialising a transfer to area A. On giving the first command to read a card into area B, it is suspended until the transfer in A is complete. The processing of card in A then takes place *at the same time* as the transfer into area B. When the processing is complete, the program is again held up until the transfer to B is finished, and then immediately proceeds to process the card in B while a transfer is being made to A. Thus the program continues, overlapping transfers and computation, and treating each card in 100 milliseconds (instead of 150). Of course the greatest gain, 50 per cent, would have occurred if the reading time and processing time had been the same. In a double-buffered system, it is always true that

> *either*, the peripheral device is driven at full speed,
>
> *or*, no computing time is lost waiting for the device.

The interrupt routine which controls any peripheral is divided into two parts. They share a common subroutine which checks that the device is operable and initiates the transfer. One part is activated whenever a user program issues a transfer extracode for the device, as shown in Fig. 9.2:

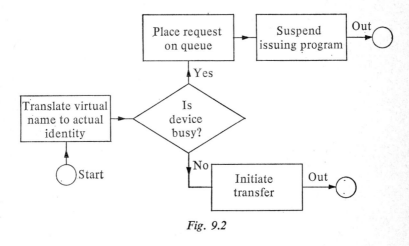

Fig. 9.2

The 'queue' referred to in Fig. 9.2 is large enough to store all the details of *one* transfer request.

The second part of the interrupt routine, of which the flow chart is shown in Fig. 9.3, is called whenever the device finishes some operation, and produces an interrupt.

On completion, both parts of the routine jump to a section of the control procedure which checks that there are no interrupts left to service, and then selects a non-suspended process to run next.

Some programs have such small quantities of input or output that it is not worth setting up a double buffer. To cope with this situation most systems have a special extracode, equivalent to a dummy transfer, which has the meaning: 'Suspend me until my device number n has finished its current transfer'.

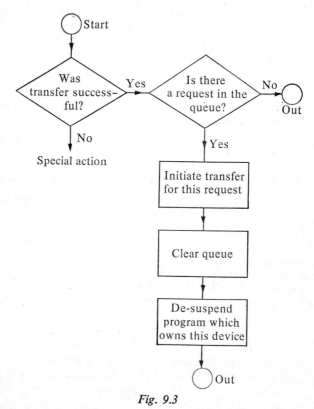

Fig. 9.3

This method of control is not really suitable for those devices which have very slow and unpredictable response times, like typewriters. This is particularly true if the program is attempting to service many of the devices at the same time. For this type of use, the programmer is given a 'virtual interrupt system'. He may initiate a transfer on any device by giving a suitable extracode, and then interrogate its state by examining the contents of a 'pseudo communication register'. The actual interrupt is simulated by an extracode which means: 'Suspend me until any one of my devices needs further attention'.

The attachment of real peripherals to users' programs is of course essential for interactive situations, and in cases where the material recorded is to be read back later by the same program. The method we have described confers the standard advantages of virtual addressing, but it lays the system open to occurrences of the 'deadly embrace' and if a program makes inefficient use of any device, by not double-buffering it or leaving it idle for long periods, the operating system can do nothing about it. There are also very severe restrictions about which programs can be allowed to run at the same time, since there have to be enough devices to satisfy the needs of all concurrent programs.

In more sophisticated systems, the input and output of non-interactive programs is often handled through 'wells'. A well is a buffer store, usually located on a random access medium like disk or drum.

The prime purpose of a well is to avoid delays by smoothing out fluctuations in demand and supply of data. A good analogy to a well is provided by a domestic water-tank supplied by a pipe of very narrow bore; provided the tank is big enough, and the *average* demand of water is not greater than the maximum the pipe can supply, peak demands can be met without any trouble.

To illustrate this concept, let us consider an output well. It consists of a number of blocks of backing store some of which are chained together on a free space list. The well contains a number of 'documents'. Each document consists of a number of records, and occupies one or more blocks. Within each block, the records are arranged sequentially, but the consecutive blocks of each document are chained together by explicit links.

In association with the well, there is a dictionary of all the documents present. Some of the documents are marked as 'complete'; others are incomplete, and each has an associated buffer, in core (Fig. 9.4). The buffer is the same size as a block in the well, and has its own pointer. In addition, each document has an indication of the device (punch, line printer, etc.) for which it is intended.

Whenever a program issues an extracode requesting the allocation of an output device, the operating system merely sets up a new document in the output well, using the identity of the program as a 'title'. It also assigns the document a core buffer and initialises a suitable pointer.

If the program now gives a transfer extracode to the device it 'thinks' it has been allocated, the output data is merely moved to the buffer, and the pointer advanced accordingly. If the pointer reaches the end of the buffer, the system takes a block from the free space list, copies the buffer into it, chains it on to previous blocks (if any), and resets the buffer pointer. If there are no free blocks in the well, the program which issued the extracode is suspended until there are.

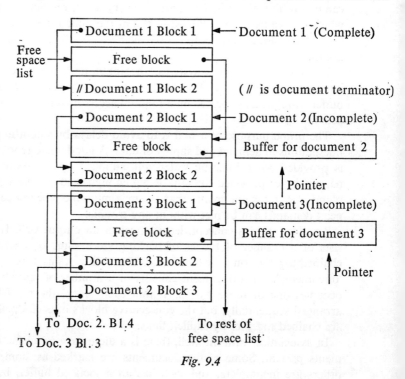

Fig. 9.4

Eventually, the program which has been producing the document is either deleted, or else gives an extracode 'releasing the device'. When this happens, the document is marked as 'complete', and the buffer space in the core is recovered.

Elsewhere in the system, there is a completely separate process for driving each output peripheral. This process scans the dictionary of the output well, looking for a complete document which is intended for that device. As soon as it finds one, it prints or punches it (suitably headed), and returns the blocks it occupied to the free space list.

It only stops if the well contains no more documents of its own kind.

The input well in an operating system is run by a highly similar method. All input destined for programs is read in advance and placed in the well. Whenever a program attempts to allocate itself an input device, it is 'attached' to a document in the input well, and reads all its data from there.

The use of input well confers three major, and one minor advantage:

First, all the peripherals are driven at full speed unless there is nothing for them to do. This generally increases the throughput of the machine, in the same way as 'off-lining' improves the work capacity of a simple batch monitor system.

Second, there need be no more constraints about which programs can run together. It is perfectly possible to run several programs all using virtual line printers at the same time, even though the whole machine only includes one real printer.

Third, most transfers are very fast, since they only involve core-to-core movement of data. This means that programs which are to be run on a system with wells need not include elaborate mechanisms for double-buffering, or other time-saving devices.

Fourth, all input passes through the operating system before being supplied to users' programs. In situations where there are many different kinds of data preparation equipment, it is often possible to carry out automatic code conversion, so that the programmer is spared the difficulty of copying with non-standard codes.

On some machines, the character codes on the various devices all conform to a common standard. Programs written for such machines do not need to specify which type of device is to be associated with any input or output stream; the connection can be made by the operating system, and can vary with different runs of the same program. Such programs are said to be 'device-independent'.

10 Filing Systems

The large majority of modern operating systems are designed to include file stores. A filing system is an arrangement for storing and maintaining a set of documents in such a way that they are easily accessible to authorised users of the machine. The operating system includes or has access to a set of procedures for setting up, editing and generally manipulating documents in any way specified by the user.

The *document* is the basic item in a file store. It consists of a set of ordered characters or records, and has an identifying name. The document can represent a wide variety of objects – it can be a program in source form, in relocatable or absolute binary: it can be a set of data; or it can be a text completely unconnected with computing, like a price list or a poem. In some systems, each document is marked with its type; however, this is restrictive, since one must usually take special action to introduce new types.

The physical representation of documents depends on the medium in which they are stored. It is universal, though, for documents to be arranged in 'blocks' of fixed length. If the document is organised on the basis of individual characters, then each block will contain a number of consecutive characters. Included in the lexicon, there will have to be characters with special meanings: for example, there must be one to indicate the end of the document. If the document is on a linear medium (like magnetic tape), then consecutive blocks can occupy adjacent positions, and there will be no need for explicit links between them; but on a random access device the blocks will be chained together, and there will have to be a special character with the meaning "the next 2 (or 3) characters must be taken together, and will give the address of the next block". If the document is organised as a sequence of records, then each record will be preceded by a warning marker, to show how long it is. The role of the 'special characters' can now be assigned to these markers. One disk system (based on 24-bit words divided into 6-bit characters) uses the following conventions:

Marker	Meaning
n	The record immediately following is n words long.
$2^{23} + b$	There are no more records in this block; the document is continued in block b.
-1	This is the end of the document.

The form of a very short document (in this convention) might be:

(Block 4)

6	MARY	▽HAD	▽A▽L	ITTL	E▽LA	MB;▽

7	ITS▽	FLEE	CE▽W	AS▽W	HITE	▽AS▽	SNOW	$2^{23}+17$

(Block 17)

8	AND▽	EVER	YWHE	RE▽T	HAT▽	MARY	▽WEN	T▽▽▽

6	THE▽	LAMB	▽WAS	▽SUR	E▽TO	▽GO.	1

(▽ IS 'SPACE' SYMBOL)

The way the whole file store is organised also depends critically on the medium used. In the past, quite effective file stores have been kept on paper tape or cards, with the identity of each document being written on to each reel or pack by the operator. Such systems are, happily, too primitive to discuss here. The simplest format currently used is for file stores on magnetic tape. If a tape contains only one document, then the identity of the document can be chosen to coincide with the name recorded on the header block of the tape. If several documents are recorded on the same physical tape, then each one must be preceded by a 'title block', which contains the appropriate name and date of creation. In most cases, the group of documents will belong to a single user. The tape is often called a 'file', and the individual documents 'subfiles'.

If a tape is of the 'industry-compatible' type, then it is impossible to write to any part of it without running the risk of making all further parts unreadable. This implies that new documents can be added to files on this kind of tape, but that existing documents cannot be deleted or altered without copying the entire tape in the process. It is also difficult to arrange for a directory of documents to be set up at the front of the tape, where it would serve a useful purpose. This snag does not arise in the case of pre-addressed tape, where blocks may be overwritten selectively, and machines which use this kind of tape (notably ATLAS and the PDP family) usually have directories at or near the front of tape files. The directories can be used to determine whether any tape actually contains a required document before it is searched; in some systems, the directories can also indicate the approximate positions of the documents, and the tape transports can be instructed to locate the tape in roughly the right place, at high speed, without actually scanning it.

A more effective way of organising a file is to store it on a random access device, such as a fixed or exchangeable disk. In this case, it is almost universal for there to be a directory. In the rare cases where the directory is absent, the entire file must be scanned whenever a named document is needed. Sometimes the directory is simply a linear list, but more often it has a two-level hierarchical structure. At the uppermost level, there is a list of users, and then at the lower level, each user has his own private directory of documents. It is very common for the 'user' entry to contain additional information, such as accounting data and possibly a 'password' which must be quoted to gain access to that user's documents.

In one system (ICLs GEORGE 3) the file store is hierarchical to an arbitrary degree. It is intended to reflect the structure of the organisation using the computer, so that one user (individual or corporate) may have several subsidiary users, who may each have even lesser users, and so ad infinitum.

Fig. 10.1 represents part of a GEORGE 3 file store as it might be set up in a university. Each user is in a rectangular block, and the actual documents, which are the terminal nodes in the graph, are shown as circles. It can be seen that the Physics Department is a user; but it has subsidiary users called 'Nuclear Physics' and 'Solid State Physics'.

The advantages conferred by this structure are chiefly in the field

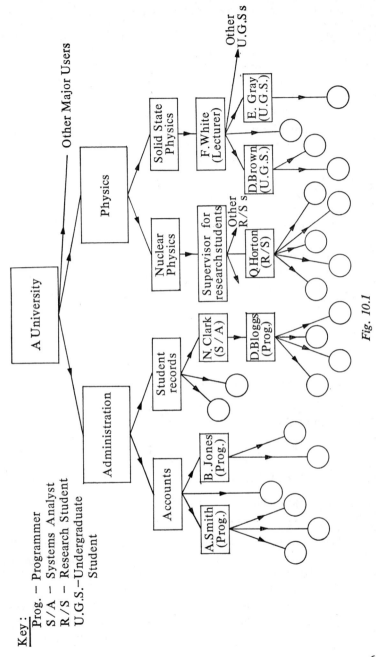

Key:
Prog. – Programmer
S/A – Systems Analyst
R/S – Research Student
U.G.S.–Undergraduate
Student

Fig. 10.1

of accounting and control of users. One disadvantage is that to reach any given document it may be necessary to chain through a whole sequence of directories.

There are various ways in which documents in the file store can be referred to by the system's users. Some systems are completely file-based. The standard command is to run document α (which is an absolute binary program) using document β as data and to call the resultant output stream γ. This same command can apply either to the execution of a previously compiled program, or to a compilation, in which case α is a compiler, β, a source text and γ the resultant object code. The user would also have subsidiary commands to manipulate individual documents, to list them on an output device or to read new versions from an input medium.

Often, programs generate their own file references automatically. For example, a compiler may refer to a library file whenever it comes across a procedure or function name which is unknown to it.

Certain systems are semi-file based. Thus, the basic form of input may be through a peripheral device, but the user can have the option of inserting the copy of a stored document, anywhere in his input, by a standard command. In the JUNE system, a document can be selected by a line of the form:

*DOLPHIN/FILE NAME. DOCUMENT NAME/

To give an example, a library procedure called DET can be put into an ALGOL program by the following sequence:

```
begin integer n; n: = read;
  begin real array a [1 :n, 1 :n];
*DOLPHIN/ALGOL LIBR. DET/

procedure f(x, yz); value x, yz;
. . . . . . . . . . . .
```

Here the word 'DOLPHIN', although an acronym, is actually chosen for its mnemonic significance. In this system, any document of any type can be inserted in this way. The method is extremely useful for supplying standard data for students' problems.

In most installations, there is a chronic shortage of space on the disk. This fact has led many systems to use multi-level file stores. Documents in frequent use are kept on a rapidly accessible medium (like bulk core or disk), and those which are not so active are relegated to a slower device – usually magnetic tape. The main difference between such systems lies in the way they are organised. At one extreme, users are absolutely free to specify where they wish their documents to reside. This is unsatisfactory, since the act of transferring a document from disk to tape is not part of the process of getting results from the computer, and most users are far too lazy to bother about doing so, even if they receive continual exhortation from the management. The outcome is that the disk soon gets cluttered with unwanted documents, and there is no room left for new users.

At the other extreme, the movement of documents between the various forms of store is entirely automatic, and is undertaken by the operating system itself. Its action is similar (in principle) to paging; whenever room is needed on the disk, the system will select and relegate that document which has been inactive for the longest period. This arrangement has the serious drawback that if a document is referred to after having been dormant for several days, it will probably be stored on a tape and may take several hours to be retrieved. This leads to the wasteful practice of 'file massage', or referring to a document at frequent intervals for no other purpose than to keep it in the fast store.

Probably, the best solution is a compromise. In some systems, the user is made responsible for organising his own storage, but is given the strongest encouragement by the accounting system to do so in an optimal manner. In other systems, the relegation is automatic, but the user is permitted to state an 'availability index' for each document, which is taken into account when the system decides whether or not to relegate.

Two very important aspects of filing systems are their *security* and *integrity*. Security is concerned with maintaining the privacy of individual documents against unauthorised reading or alteration. In simple systems, there is little need for special security measures. Provided that there is no general motive for prying into other users' documents, it is sufficient for any user with a private document not to let its name be generally known. Since all access to documents is through their names, this gives sufficient protection.

In more complex systems, each user has a secret password, as we explained above. The arrangement for supplying this password is such as to encourage secrecy; for example if it is supplied with a pack

65

of cards, then the password need not be near the beginning but can be inserted anywhere; or if input on a teletype, it is either not 'echoed back', or else the operating system makes arrangements for it to be printed over a jumble of erase characters, so that it is not legible.

At still higher levels of security, systems distinguish between four kinds of access to documents:

(a) complete access – (for reading, altering, obeying or deleting);
(b) read-only access (for reading and obeying only);
(c) obey-only access (the user can obey this document as a program, but may neither read nor alter it);
(d) all access barred.

This kind of distinction is apposite in a commercial time-sharing bureau. A user is allowed to read and alter documents in his own file. He can read (but not alter) the file which contains the records of his use of the system. He can call and obey certain standard programs, but he is not allowed even to list them (in case he were to sell them to a rival bureau). The files of other customers are closed to him entirely.

With these levels of access, it is clearly necessary to have several levels of user, some with special privileges. One would expect the manager of the installation to have complete control over all the files. The programmers at the bureau would be allowed to read and alter the standard programs, and the accounting section would have access to all the use records.

If taken to its logical limit, this approach leads to the situation where each user is in a unique relationship to all the others, and is allowed to specify who may read his files, or use the programs in them. The set of relationships can be expressed as a matrix, thus:

		User				
		1	2	3	4	5
User	1	a	d	c	d	d
	2	d	a	c	b	d
	3	b	b	a	b	b
	4	a	d	c	a	d
	5	a	a	a	a	a

(here user 1 may obey 3's programs; user 2 may obey 3's programs and read 4's documents; user 5 has complete access to all documents, but is secure from all prying except from 3.)

The integrity of a filing system is a measure of its ability to recover after hardware failures which corrupt part of the storage system. If serious use is to be made of a file store, it is essential that the users have some sort of guarantee that their documents, which may represent a great deal of work, will not simply vanish at the first disk crash.

The requirement of integrity can only be achieved by storing information twice over. In a system with a sufficiently small file store (less than, say, 5 million characters) it is possible to copy the whole of the file store on to magnetic tape at regular intervals. The only information to be lost in the event of a catastrophe will be that which was recorded after the most recent dump.

Where the fast storage medium is larger, total dumps are no longer economically feasible. The system used is called 'incremental dumping', and consists of periodically recording all the documents which have changed since the last incremental dump.

An essential part of the integrity system consists of a number of house-keeping programs. In a context of total dumping, it is sufficient to have a method of reconstructing the disk store from the most recent tape. With incremental dumping, numerous dump tapes have to be read to reset the system. It is clearly impossible to store and then read *all* the incremental dumps ever produced since the system was first started, so periodically all the archive tapes older than a certain number of days have to be consolidated together into one 'summary', or 'base' tape. The necessary software is made even more complicated because the archives have to be protected against accidental damage while the tapes are being used to reset the system or being consolidated. It turns out that the maintenance of a file store is a time-consuming activity, and may take up a substantial proportion of the complete system's resources.

We shall end this chapter with an illustrative example. The DOLPHIN filing system uses total dumping, but combines the functions of providing integrity and of providing a two-level system in one operation.

As far as the user is aware, the system may contain several of his documents. Each one is either immediately available (that is on the disk) or 'banished' (that is on magnetic tape). At any time, the user can create a new document on the disk, or he may delete one from the disk. He may also specify that a named document, now on the

67

disk, is to be banished, or relegated to the tape, and he may request that a previously banished document be retrieved.

In actual fact, the dump tape contains copies of all the documents in the system, including those which are supposed to be on the disk. At regular intervals (once a day) the previous day's tape is processed to make a new one. The process is as follows:

First, the system makes an ordered list of all the documents it knows about, including all those actually on the disk, and the names of those which have been deleted, or for which a request for retrieval has been made. Next, the old dump tape is read, and the names of the documents it contains merged with the ordered list. Each document is noted as being either in, or else out of, five independent categories:

A: on the old dump tape
B: on the disk
C: having been deleted
D: marked for banishment
E: marked for retrieval

Out of the thirty-two combinations, all are possible except the one where a document is a member of no category, because in this case it would not be known to the system. Out of the remaining 31, 13 are 'sensible', and the other 18 can easily arise due to human errors in giving document names. The action taken for each document, as the old dump tape is scanned, depends on the exact combination of categories. Some examples are:

A only: This is simply a banished document which is to remain banished. It is copied to the output dump tape.

A and B: This is a document which is currently residing on the disk, and may have been changed since the last dump. The disk version is copied to the output tape, and the version on the input tape is skipped.

A, B and D: This document is now marked for banishment. The new version is copied to the output tape and then erased from the disk; the old version on the input tape is skipped.

68

E only: Here the user has asked for a non-existent document
            to be retrieved. A fault message is printed.

In the next chapter, we shall discuss the design and construction of editors and other programs used to construct and alter documents in the file store.

11 Filing and Editing

In this chapter we shall consider the various operations which are often lumped together under the headings of 'filing' and 'editing'. The procedures which implement these operations can be organised in different ways; sometimes they form an integral part of the operating system itself, sometimes they are the task of a special program which has privileged access to the file store, but otherwise has the same status as a user's program; and sometimes editing and filing functions form part of the repertoire of a special utility program such as an on-line compiler.

In general, filing functions are those which are concerned with the manipulation of complete documents. A basic set of functions must include the following:

    (a) Reading new documents from peripherals (including a teletype console).
    (b) Listing documents on output devices (including a console).
    (c) Copying documents within the store.
    (d) Deleting documents from the file store.

Some filing systems offer further facilities. Three possible additions to this list are,

    (e) Renaming an existing document.
    (f) Joining two documents together.
    (g) Justifying a document (or arranging it into lines of constant width, as far as possible).

When a user specifies a filing operation, he always does so in the form of a 'function call' with 'parameters', although this may be syntactically disguised. Thus we have in the DOLPHIN system,

    READ SIMEQ, TR

which is a command to read a document called 'SIMEQ' from a tape reader.

In GEORGE 3, the corresponding command is,

    INPUT SIMEQ, GRAPHIC, TZZZZ

where GRAPHIC indicates the mode (or convention) in which the document is punched, and TZZZZ is the sequence by which the document ends. (In DOLPHIN, the terminating sequence is given at the head of the document itself).

In the PDP/10 system, the command is quite simply,

MAKE SIMEQ

Here it is assumed that the text of the new document will follow on the device on which the command itself was read. The document will end with a terminator standard to the system.

The way in which these functions are implemented depends on the general organisation of the file store. Where a disk is used, there will be a list of free blocks from which space will be taken as needed, and to which blocks will be returned when a document is deleted. In systems where there is an acute lack of core storage, the blocks in the free space list may actually be chained together. This leads to the difficulty that the blocks soon lose their natural ordering, and consecutive blocks in the free space list (and therefore in any newly created document) will come from widely separated areas of the disk store. Such documents are wasteful and time-consuming to handle on a disk drive with movable heads. This difficulty can be overcome, at the cost of some core store, by maintaining a disk 'map', with one bit for each block, showing which of the blocks are currently free. It is then possible for the system to arrange new documents in groups of adjacent blocks.

When considered over many systems, filing functions have a certain uniformity. This is emphatically not the case with editing functions, which are designed to make alterations within documents. Major differences between editing systems arise in several areas; for example, some systems are intended for batch mode processing, others for conversational use; some indicate the positions of amendments by line number, and some by context; some edit an existing document *in situ*, while others merge an old document with a set of amendments to produce a distinct new document.

To a large extent, these differences are due to the various contexts in which the systems work. In a batch-mode editor, the user cannot see what the immediate effect his amendments are having, so it is important to have an absolutely unambiguous way of specifying alterations in advance. On the other hand, teletypes and visual display units allow the editing process to be monitored at all stages, so

71

that a system based on either of these devices can be much more relaxed.

To illustrate these ideas we shall describe several representative systems.

A good example of a primitive but effective batch mode editor is ICL's COSY system. This is used for amending source program in assembly code. In the file store (which may be on tape or disk), each line of code is effectively labelled by its line number.

The numbers, which are consecutive, are not actually stored but generated whenever they are needed. Every time a program is assembled, the line numbers are printed on the listing. The editor program understands only one type of amendment order:

$$\text{\# ALTER} \quad m, n$$
$$\left.\begin{array}{l} \text{------} \\ \text{------} \\ \text{------} \end{array}\right\} \text{ Lines of new code}$$

This means, 'Remove the n lines starting at line m, and insert the new lines given'. There is no danger of confusion because in the assembly language it is impossible for a valid line to begin with the characters # ALTER. It is permitted for there to be no new lines of code – in which case the amendment is simply a deletion. n may also be zero, which makes the amendment into an insertion, conventionally *before* line m.

The system works by merging the old document and list of amendments to generate a new document. This implies that if there is more than one amendment, they must be supplied in increasing order of line numbers. This restriction is not onerous, and the system is well suited to implementing changes which have been planned in advance on a listing of the previous compilation of the program. The only drawback – and it is not a serious one – is that as a program goes through several versions, the line numbers of instructions tend to change. It is therefore disastrous to base one's amendments on any listing except the most recent.

Another example of a line-based system is offered by the BASIC system. BASIC is a simple algorithmic language designed for interactive use. The special system available on most machines includes an editor and a compiler which are closely integrated. Initially, the user is invited to type his program and data, preceding each line with a line number of his own choice. Generally, the line numbers go up in steps of 10. When the program is complete, the user gives the command RUN (without a line number), and the system compiles and runs the program. Before it does so, it sorts the lines into ascending order, and where two or more lines have the same number, it takes only the last one into account. This implies that the user, if he makes a mistake, can correct it without retyping the whole program. An example is given below:

```
10   READ N
20   LET A = 0
30   LTE
30   LET S 0
40   READ Q
50   LET A = A + 1
60   LET S = S + Q
70   IF A < N GOTO 40
80   PRINT R
75   LET R = S/A
90   END
77   PRINT 'AVERAGE IS'
30   LET S = 0
RUN
```

This is precisely equivalent to

```
10   READ N
20   LET A = 0
30   LET S = 0
40   READ Q
50   LET A = A + 1
60   LET S = S + Q
70   IF A < N GOTO 40
75   LET R = S/A
77   PRINT 'AVERAGE IS'
80   PRINT R
90   END
```

One defect of this particular program is that it lacks any data. The command RUN will make the system type an error message. The user will then be able to correct his program, and run it again by typing:

> 100 DATA 5, 2, 4, 7, 5, 3
> RUN

This time, the job will run correctly, and produce the output,

> AVERAGE IS
> 4·20000

If the user is satisfied with his program, he may give an instruction for it to be given a name and inserted into the permanent file store.

Next, we shall discuss editors which depend on context for locating the areas to be amended. We shall illustrate the various principles by reference to three different practical systems: ICL's GEORGE 3, the DOLPHIN editor (developed at Lancaster University) and TECO, developed for the PDP/6 at M.I.T. and now supported by the Digital Equipment Corporation.

The GEORGE 3 editor (which is an integral part of the operating system) works on the principle of scanning the input text and creating a distinct 'output' document which incorporates the necessary amendments. The system is primarily designed to handle complete lines as units, although changes within lines are also possible.

When editing starts, the original text is given a 'pointer', which is positioned at the beginning. Editing proceeds by a series of steps, in which commands to make amendments alternate with commands to move the pointer to the place where the next change is to be made. Every time the pointer is moved, the text which is skipped is copied to the 'output' document.

The pointer commands may, but need not, depend on context. Some of them are:

/FIND 50 FORMAT   (The pointer is moved to the beginning of the first line to start '50 FORMAT').

/LOCATE 'END' OF   (The pointer is moved to the beginning of the first line to contain the sequence ' 'END' OF ').

/BOTTOM   (The pointer is moved to the end of the document).

Once the pointer has been positioned, n lines can be deleted by the command,

/ALTER N

and new lines can be inserted (at the same place, if necessary) simply by typing them. All lines not preceded by a warning character (which we have arbitrarily selected as /) are taken as new text to be sent to the output document.

The system also allows changes to be made within lines by quoting the string of characters to be removed and giving another string to replace it.

Finally, the editing process can be terminated by the command

/END

This system is efficient and simple in operation and powerful enough to permit source programs and data documents to be edited without series of complicated commands. Its chief drawback is that it is not possible to interchange the order of sections of the document without erasing and then retyping at least one of them.

The DOLPHIN system, where the emphasis is on alterations at the character level, overcomes these difficulties at the cost of considerable complexity in its software. Here, there are no 'input' and 'output' documents, but the original text is modified *in situ*. Within the Dolphin program (but not directly accessible to the user) are two routines called MATCH and PATCH. Initially, a general pointer (which is called '*') is affixed to the beginning of the document being edited. Routine MATCH takes a string as argument, and starting from the current position of *, scans the document until it finds an occurrence of the string. It then produces two results, which are pointers delimiting the occurrence. Routine PATCH uses a piece of text and two pointers as parameters. It deletes the section of the document between the pointers and replaces it by the given text.

The various instructions available to the user of Dolphin nearly all

75

make use of one or other of these two routines. The user is aware of his main pointer (*) and of 26 ancillary pointers called A to Z. At any time, any of the pointers can be set to the beginning of the document (or moved back there) by a command of the form

> pointer = 0
> (for example A = 0 or * = 0)

The basic pointer setting instruction is

> pointer (1) = "quotation" = pointer (2)
> (for example A = "HD(L) + HD(TL(L))" = Z)

Here the text is scanned by MATCH, and its results are assigned to the two named pointers. Truncated forms of the instruction, such as

> A = "FUNCTION QB"

and "THE END" = B

are permitted and commonly used.

The fundamental form of the instruction which actually alters the document is

> segment (1) = segment (2)

The implication is that segment (1) is to be replaced by segment (2). The first segment may be a section of the text defined by an ordered pointer pair, or it may be a quotation, in which case MATCH is automatically called in to locate it. The second segment may be a quotation, or it may be a copy of a section of the document defined by a pointer pair, or it can be a concatenation of either of these joined by +.

When using Dolphin small alterations can be made by commands like,

> "a : = a + 1" = "a : = a − 1"

When making larger amendments, sections of the file to be deleted are usually marked by pointers so that they need not be quoted in full. For example:

> A   = " 'procedure' F(x)"
>   " 'end' of procedure F;" = B
> AB = " 'procedure' F(x,y);
> ------
>
> ------
>   'end' of procedure F(x,y);"

To interchange two sections of a document, one first marks them with pointers, thus:

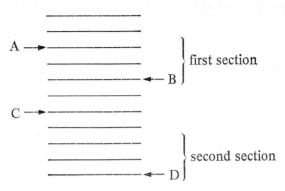

The rearrangement can now be made by the single command

$$AD = CD + BC + AB$$

In general, the documents handled by DOLPHIN are far too large to fit completely into the core store. Editing must be done with the document still on the disk, with several blocks 'paged' into the core, although this paging is done automatically and is hidden from the user. Under these circumstances, it is not possible to overwrite material which is deleted with new text, because there may not be enough room for it. The new text has to be stored in a special 'amendments' area and connected to the rest of the document by explicit links. Since the links point only one way, the pointer cannot be moved backwards (except to the beginning of the document).

Another solution to this problem is offered by the TECO editor. It is recognised that a text which is completely in the core store is much easier to manipulate because it can be stored as a linear array of characters without any links. Pointers can be moved in either direction, and new material can be inserted in its right place by moving the following text up or down as necessary. (This would be impossibly time-consuming on a disk).

The TECO system works by reading sections called 'pages' from an input document, altering them (if necessary) and writing them to an output document. While each page is in the core store, it is amended *in situ*; a very wide variety of instructions is provided, including various pointer setters (line number and context) commands for inserting and deleting text, and orders for reading and writing the pages. There are special facilities for setting up and obeying a 'stored program' of editing commands.

The TECO system has been adapted for use with a visual display. When a page is displayed on a cathode ray tube, the position for the next amendment can be chosen by pointing with a light pen or a cursor – this is much easier than counting lines or specifying a context.

It appears that different types of users like editors with varying degrees of sophistication. Occasional computer users will tend to use very simple systems, even though they may lack certain facilities. To cope with this demand it is quite common for installations to provide several different editors and to give their users a completely free choice.

12 Job Descriptions

When an operating system runs a job, it does so by carrying out a set of primitive operations which are effectively specified by a 'job description' in the batch mode, or by a series of 'monitor commands' if in the multi-access regime. The primitives are carried out by a section of the operating system called the 'job control'.

We started our discussion by describing the primitive operations used by most systems. We shall assign each operation a 'conventional representation', so that we can easily refer to that type of operation again. It must be understood that this form is not necessarily that used in any existing system.

The primitives fall into several groups. The first group is concerned with the direct control of programs:

'LOAD XYZ'   This command fetches the absolute binary program called XYZ from the file store, and loads it ready for running. The new program may overwrite any previous program which may have been loaded for this job.

'GO'   The program which has been loaded is activated. It will keep running, without intervention from the 'job control' section of the operating system, until an 'event' occurs. This may either be an internal event, occasioned by an 'end of run' extracode issued by the program itself, or it may be an event initiated externally, by part of the operating system, because one or other of the resources assigned to the job (such as mill time) has run out. Whenever an event takes place, the operating system is always supplied with enough information to determine its cause.

The second group of primitive operations is used to implement the mechanisms for device-independent input and output. As we explained in a previous chapter, a device-independent program is one which refers to 'channel numbers' rather than to any specific type of peripheral device; this makes it possible to use it under a wide variety of conditions.

INPUT n = DEVICE
(for example, INPUT 4 = CARD READER)

Here, the operating system sets up a mechanism which ensures that whenever the user's program calls for a record on channel n, the next record in the stream on the correct device is supplied. The device may be coupled to the program either directly, or – more commonly – through an input well. If an input well is used, special precautions – such as naming the document – are necessary to ensure that the right input stream is selected.

INPUT n = DOCUMENT NAME
(for example, INPUT 1 = SURVEY DATA)

This form is used if the input stream is to be taken from a document already in the file store. When obeying this operation, the operating system sets up the appropriate buffers and pointers.

OUTPUT n = DEVICE
(for example, OUTPUT 0 = LINE PRINTER)

> This operation is the exact converse of one described above. The peripheral named is either attached to the program directly, or else a new document is opened in the output well. Any output which the program produces on this channel is handled appropriately.

OUTPUT n = DOCUMENT NAME
(for example, OUTPUT 3 = BINPROG)

> This operation is used to set up a document in the file store as an output stream. The operating system first checks whether a document of this name already exists; if so, it erases it. It then creates a new document of the required name, and arranges for all output on the specified channel number to be appended to this document.

Whenever a program in the sequence forming a job is over-written by another one, or when a job is ended, all the input and output channels are closed. Any peripherals used on-line are freed; documents in the input well are erased, documents in the output well are marked as 'complete' so that they can eventually be output, and new files are closed (but not deleted).

Next we have two important ancillary instructions:

SEND 'MESSAGE'
(for example, SEND 'YOUR PROGRAM CONTAINED ERRORS')

> Here, the given message is transmitted to the user.

FINISH

> This signifies that the job as a whole has ended. The operating system deletes it, issues an accoun-

81

ting record, and returns all the resources used by the job to the
central pool.

The commands we have given are quite sufficient for running jobs
in the multi-access mode. The user can steer his job through the system manually, giving the necessary commands one by one.

For batch mode running, all the commands have to be given in
advance, so that they can be stored and obeyed automatically. The
sequence of commands now acquires the status of a primitive 'stored
program', and we can introduce jump instructions, which discrimi-
nate on the reasons for events, and a labelling system for all instructions. We write jump instructions as:

> IF CONDITION THEN GOTO n
> (for example, 'IF MILL TIME ALLOWANCE RUN OUT
> THEN GOTO 5')

The last group of primitive operations is concerned with setting
resource limits. Each of these operations is carried out at the beginning of a job, but it makes the system keep a constant 'watch'. An
event can be initiated at any time, if the resource limits are indeed
violated. The limits are checked by those parts of the system responsible for running individual programs.

We write the resource limit operations as

> SET TIME $= n$
> SET OUTPUT LIMIT $m = n$ (limit of n lines on channel m)
> SET SPACE $= n$ (This is only useful in
> systems where programs
> are allowed to vary their
> own size. It sets a limit to
> the amount of storage
> used)

The number of basic operations needed to run any job depends on
the degree to which the standard programs help the operating system.
On the ATLAS, which we shall consider first, the compilers do a
great deal more than on other systems. Each compiler produces absolute binary object code which it dumps, correctly positioned, into one
of its work areas. This presents no particular storage problems, be-

cause all programs in ATLAS work in a virtual store of about a million words, which is always enough room for both the compiler and the object code generated. If the source code of a program is correct, the compiler then erases itself (except for standard routines used at run time) and transfers control to the object program. It can be said that the compiler 'turns itself into' the program it has compiled. All this is achieved without significant intervention of the job control level of the operating system.

The sequence of primitive operations which the ATLAS operating system carries out for each job is fixed. The job description consists of a sequence of *indicative* statements, which specify values for the various parameters of the operations. A typical job description might be:

JOB VL999 Q. BLOGGS	(Title and identification)
COMPUTING 100 SECONDS	(Maximum mill time allowance)
OUTPUT 0 LINEPRINTER 2000 LINES	(Definition of output channel and maximum quantity of output).
STORE 70 BLOCKS	(Maximum store allowance: 1 block is 512 words)
COMPILER ALGOL	(Compiler to be used)

This job description would normally be followed by a program, data (if applicable)) and a standard terminator, '***Z'.

The sequence of operations obeyed for this job is shown below. Actual parameters are substituted in the obvious ways:

LOAD ALGOL	
INPUT 0 = SELF	(This refers to the remainder of the document on which the job description was punched)
OUTPUT 0 = LINE PRINTER	
SET TIME = 100	
SET SPACE = 70	
SET OUTPUT LIMIT 0 = 2000	
GO	
FINISH	

On most other systems, the compilers do far less than on ATLAS. In systems which use pure procedures, it is of course impossible for a compiler to 'turn itself into' anything else. Recent systems pay a great deal of attention to the concept of 'mixed language programming', and this means that the compilers must generate relocatable binary code which can subsequently be combined with code produced by different compilers. Normally, the relocatable binary code is generated in the form of an output stream; before it can be run, it has to be processed by another program called 'a consolidator' or 'link loader' which fills in the necessary external code (usually from a program library) and converts the whole program to absolute binary. Usually, (but not always) the link loader is able to turn itself into the program it has just assembled without operating system intervention.

The sequence of commands needed to run even a simple FORTRAN job in batch mode is unexpectedly large. In the following example, we assume that the file store already contains two documents called PROGRAM and DATA, and that output is to be sent to the line printer. The values for resource limits and channel number have been chosen arbitrarily.

The sequence is:

```
            SET TIME = 1000
            SET OUTPUT LIMIT 0 = 5000
            SET SPACE = 15000
            LOAD FORTRAN              (Fetch the FORTRAN
                                       compiler)
            OUTPUT 0 = LINE PRINTER
                                      (For listing)
            OUTPUT 1 = REL-BIN        (Assign output document
                                       in file store for relocat-
                                       able binary output)
            INPUT 0 = PROGRAM
            GO                        (Activate compiler)
            IF TIME RUN OUT THEN GOTO 1
                                      (Obeyed only when an
                                       event has stopped the
                                       compiler)
            IF SPACE RUN OUT THEN GOTO 2
            IF OUTPUT ALLOWANCE RUN OUT THEN GOTO 3
            IF COMPILATION CORRECT GOTO 4
```

```
    SEND 'ERRORS IN COMPILATION'
    FINISH
4 LOAD CONSOLIDATOR
    INPUT 0 = DATA
    INPUT 1 = REL-BIN
    OUTPUT 0 = LINE PRINTER
    GO                          (Activate consolidator,
                                which turns itself into the
                                object program)
    IF TIME RUN OUT THEN GOTO 1
    IF SPACE RUN OUT THEN GOTO 2
    IF OUTPUT ALLOWANCE RUN OUT THEN GOTO 3
    SEND 'JOB COMPLETED CORRECTLY'
    FINISH
1 SEND 'TIME ALLOWANCE EXCEEDED'
    FINISH
2 SEND 'SPACE ALLOWANCE EXCEEDED'
    FINISH
3 SEND 'PRINTING ALLOWANCE EXCEEDED'
    FINISH
```

There are various ways in which the job control section receives the coded message which indicates the reason for any event. In the IBM 360 operating system (D.O.S.) each program, when it ends, leaves a 'communication word' in one of its accumulators. The ICL 1900 system was originally designed for manual operation, and all programs are supposed to interface with human operators. Whenever an event occurs, a program produces a text message, which would have been displayed on a typewriter console but is passed to the operating system as a string instead.

The GEORGE 3 operating system allows the user to write extremely complicated job descriptions. To allow certain operations or groups of operations to be repeated several times, it includes simple arithmetic and testing facilities among its primitive commands. A job is allowed to interact with its own job description; for example, it may issue the next command to be obeyed by the job control, or it may inquire what the next one in the list will be.

A serious drawback of this type of job description is its length. It may be acceptable for a professional programmer to write a full job description for a program which is to be used many times, but it is

85

not reasonable for a student to have to precede his first program with 20 lines of what must appear to be gibberish. In the ATLAS system, this problem does not arise, since each line in the job description has an obvious and significant meaning. In other systems, the problem is usually solved by the use of 'system macros' or similar devices. A system macro is a string of job description commands with a name and with 'blanks' or formal parameters in places where the user has to supply the actual values.

When giving his job description, the user is free to specify the name of any system macro, together with the actual values for the parameter. For instance, he might put

FORTRAN (1000, 2000, 70, PROGRAM DATA)

to generate exactly the job description which we gave a few pages back.

Most operating systems give rather more flexibility in the way parameters are written. Some systems would accept this kind of format:

TIME 1000
OUTPUT 2000
SPACE 70
PROG.IDENT = PROGRAM
DATA.IDENT = DATA

Since each parameter is effectively labelled, the order in which they are given is not significant. It is usually possible to leave certain parameters out, and the system will substitute default values selected by the computer manager. The simplest job descriptions usually contain just two items – the user's identity and the compiler to be used.

Most job descriptions include lines which do not correspond directly to any of the primitive commands. Thus, it is universal for jobs to start with a title card or line which gives the identity of the user. This information is stored, and used to label the output from the job. If the machine has an internal list of users, the table can be checked to ensure that the user's name is on the list.

Job descriptions also include information which is useful to the scheduler in deciding which job to run next. This includes descriptions of any special peripheral requirements (such as named magnetic tapes or pre-printed stationery) and of any privileged status the user may have, *vis-a-vis* other users.

86

13 Multi-access

In the first few chapters of this book, we have discussed some of the principles and techniques used in modern operating systems. In most cases, we have made little distinction between batch-mode and multi-access processing, because the same basic principles are applicable to both. There is, however, a set of very real problems which do not arise in batch processing, but which must be solved if satisfactory multi-access is to be provided economically.

In a system devoted to batch mode processing, the operating system has complete control over all activities; it is free to start and then interrupt various programs in any way which will optimise the overall use of the machine. A multi-access system, however, has the important additional requirement that it has to give all its users a reasonable 'response time'; it cannot postpone the servicing of users' requests, even if their jobs may be inconvenient to carry out at that moment.

The two basic requirements – overall efficiency and good response time – are essentially antagonistic. The system designer cannot satisfy one requirement except at the expense of the other, and he has to take an engineer's decision about which type of compromise he can adopt. Fortunately, there are several ways of improving one aspect of a multi-access system without doing too much damage to the other, and it is these methods with which this chapter is largely concerned.

To begin our discussion, we reproduce, in full, a typical multi-access session on a modern system (the PDP/10). The user creates a FORTRAN program, compiles, loads and tests it in one uninterrupted sequence lasting about 10 minutes.

We notice that the whole session takes the form of a dialogue between the user and the machine. The conversation takes place at two different levels. Initially, and again at various points throughout the session, the user is giving commands directly to the system itself; for example, the statement

EXECUTE FACTOR . F40

```
LOGIN
  JOB 5     XXX. 4S72.AM 12-113-70
  ID: BLOGGS

  PASSWORD:
  ██████████

  ACCT REF: 12345
  TTY4    1740      04-JAN-71
```
Log in

```
.CREATE FACTOR.F40

*I
00010        1 FORMAT(I7)
00020        2 FORMAT(L7H THE FACTORS OF    I7)
00030        3 FORMAT(15H FACTOR PROGRAM /)
00040        4 TYPE 3
00050          ACCEPT 1,N
00060          IF (N) 7,8,7
00070        7 TYPE 2,N
00080          J=N/2
00090          DO 5 K=2,J
00100          IF(N-N/K*K)5,6,5
00110          TYPE 1,K
00120        5 CONTINUE
00130          GOTO 4
00140        8 TYPE 9
00150        9 FORMAT(16H  END OF PROGRAM)
00160          END
00170    Σ
*E
*↑C
```
Create first version of program

```
.EXECUTE FACTOR.F40
FORTRAN:  FACTOR.F40
********00020        2 FORMAT(L7H THE FACTORS OF    I7)
********                                     '
********              S-1 SYNTAX

UNDEFINED LBLS

6
MAIN.   ERRORS DETECTED: 2

? TOTAL ERRORS DETECTED: 2
```
Attempt to run it

```
.EDIT FACTOR.F40
*I20
00020'       2 FORMAT(17H THE FACTORS OF    I7)
00030'   Σ
*I110
00110'       6 TYPE 1,K
00120'   Σ
*E
*↑C
```
Correct the errors (by replacing lines 20 and 110)

88

```
•TYPE FACTOR.F40
00010        1 FORMAT(I7)
00020        2 FORMAT(17H THE FACTORS OF    I7)
00030        3 FORMAT(15H FACTOR PROGRAM /)
00040        4 TYPE 3
00050          ACCEPT 1,N
00060          IF (N) 7,8,7
00070        7 TYPE 2,N
00080          J=N/2
00090          DO 5 K=2,J
00100          IF(N-N/K*K)5,6,5
00110        6 TYPE 1,K
00120        5 CONTINUE
00130          GOTO 4
00140        8 TYPE 9
00150        9 FORMAT(16H  END OF PROGRAM)
00160          END
```

List the corrected program

```
•EXECUTE FACTOR.F40
FORTRAN:   FACTOR.F40
LOADING

LOADER 4K CORE
EXECUTION

FACTOR PROGRAM
    123

THE FACTORS OF        123
    3
    41
FACTOR PROGRAM
    1234

THE FACTORS OF        1234
    2
    617
FACTOR PROGRAM
    12345

THE FACTORS OF        12345
    3
    5
    15
    823
    2469
    4115
```

Run it

```
FACTOR PROGRAM
    120                                              Run it
THE FACTORS OF        120
        2
        3
        4
        5
        6
        8
       10
       12
      ·15
       20
       24
       30
       40
       60
FACTOR PROGRAM
        0

  END OF PROGRAM

EXECUTION TIME:        0·64 SEC·           Logging
TOTAL ELAPSED TIME:    1 MIN· 28·86 SEC·   information
NO EXECUTION ERRORS DETECTED

EXIT
↑C

·KJOB

OFF  USR BLOGGS, JOB 5    TTY4    1750    4-JAN-71   Log off
ANOTHER JOB STILL LOGGED IN UNDER [BLOGGS]
RUNTIME 0 MIN, 04·54 SEC
```

is an instruction to the system to carry out one of its elementary functions, namely to load the FORTRAN compiler. At other times, the user is in conversation with various programs which are controlled by the operating system, but are not themselves part of it. Thus, the line

12345

is data supplied to the user's own program.

Communication at the operating system level is relatively easy to achieve economically. Each user has his own message buffer, only a few words long. When the system is awaiting a command, this buffer is gradually filled, as the user types, by the interrupt routine which services the user's console. When the routine detects the end of the command, it initiates a process which analyses and eventually obeys the order. This process can be driven by a pure procedure which is capable of servicing other users at the same time. The primitive operations are all either very fast, or else are obviously limited by peripheral speeds, so there are no serious problems, either of speed or of core store requirements in servicing a large number of users simultaneously.

The economic provision of direct access to a user's own program is much harder to manage. Since the program is, in general, unique, it cannot be shared with other users and may occupy a large fraction of the whole system to the exclusion of other jobs. Furthermore, there is no guarantee that once a program receives a message from the user, it will not continue to calculate indefinitely without ever producing a result and asking for another message.

As a starting point, let us consider the design of a naive multi-access system. It has a very large core store, so large that it can hold an individual program for every active user. Each job is represented by a process which may be in one of three states:

suspended (waiting for a message from the user)

active (actually being run by the central processor)

queued (not suspended, but not active)

If there are very few jobs, the system spends most of its time waiting for messages. As soon as one arrives, the corresponding process is activated, and is allowed to run until it suspends itself after having asked for another message. As the number of users builds up, messages begin to arrive while the central processor is busy. They are placed in a queue by an interrupt routine, and are dealt with, in their order of arrival, after the current process has been suspended. The response time, which was good with small numbers of users, gets gradually worse until the central processor is busy the whole time; after this it gets rapidly worse with increasing numbers of users.

This system is unsatisfactory in two respects. First, it would need such a large core store that it would be only a little more expensive to give each user his own computer. At any moment, only a small fraction of the store would be active, the rest being locked out and idle. Second, the response time would sometimes be very long; if one user initiated a time-consuming step (like finding the millionth prime number) *all* the other users would be held up until the step was complete.

The cure to the second problem is the easier one, so we shall discuss it first. The most widely used method of keeping the response time down is to divide the time of the central processor into 'quanta' usually of about 1/10 second each. As soon as any process initiated by a user has taken up a whole quantum, it is suspended even though it may not have completed its job, and placed at the back of the queue. This ensures that users who are sending messages which are easily handled (like lines to be appended to documents in the file store) will get a good response, but users who are doing large calculations may have to wait a long time. It is, however, impossible for one user to monopolise the whole machine to the exclusion of others.

A possible variant of this system is to apply this 'round robin' rule only to users in contact with their own programs. Commands to the monitor are given an altogether high priority, being handled in a way analogous to interrupts.

Even though this system ensures against excessively long response times, it is clear that limiting factors to the speed of response are the number of users, the type of work they are doing, and the speed of the central processor.

The problem of reducing the amount of core store needed to run a multi-access system can be tackled in several ways.

The most obvious method is to use a backing store to contain those jobs which are not currently active. As soon as a new job is created, it is assigned to a permanent 'home' on a random access device such as a disk or drum, preferably with fixed heads so as to minimise access time. Whenever that job is actually run, it is read down into the core store first, and when the run ends (either because the step has been completed or because the quantum of time has run out) the job is copied back to the backing store. This technique is called 'core swapping'. On some of the earliest multi-access systems, there was only enough room in the core store for one job. A swap had to be made for every program change, and, as can be imagined, this meant that the system spent a very large part of the time doing core-to-disk transfers.

Many more recent systems permit several jobs to be present in the core store at the same time. Here, a swap only takes place if the job to be started next is not already in the core. The performance of these systems depends on the number of active users. If this is less or equal to the number of jobs which can fit into the core, the response time is good, but as the number of users increases beyond that point, swapping becomes more and more frequent, until the response time is no better than that of a system where swapping is forced every time. This is shown diagrammatically below:

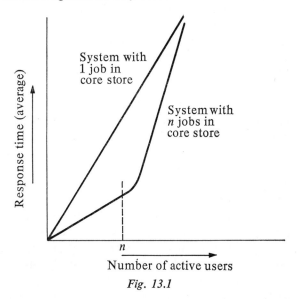

Fig. 13.1

In many cases, the system does not force a fixed size on each job, but permits it to take as much core as it needs. The number of jobs actually in the core store can therefore be a variable quantity.

There are systems in which the principle of core swapping is modified by the use of a paging mechanism. Here, all the jobs are kept in a large virtual store which has apparently only one level. The system which switches control between jobs behaves as if all the jobs were in the core store, and the actual transfers between core and disk are carried out by part of the paging mechanism, as described in Chapter 5. This can result in a substantial saving of time because in many cases it is not necessary to bring the whole of a job into the core store, but only those blocks which are actually referred to during some particular step or quantum.

One of the most significant advances in improving the efficiency of multi-access systems is the use of standard programs, such as editors and compilers, in the form of pure procedures. This means that only one copy of a program need be held in the store, irrespective of the number of jobs actually using it. The only areas which need be particular for each user are those which contain his data. In a system without re-entrant standard programs, the storage requirements for a program such as an editor might be 5K per user; with the facility, it would still be 5K for the first user, but only, say, 1K for each additional one. Many more active users can be squeezed into the core store before any swapping becomes necessary, and even when it starts, it will be fast because only the relatively small data areas need be swapped.

Pure procedures are most easily implemented on machines which have dual relocation registers or paging mechanisms. They can be written for machines without these facilities, but the result is always more clumsy; for example, every data reference must be modified by a special index register reserved for this purpose, or the complete data area must be swapped in and out of a given (fixed) area every time that the procedure is transferred from one job to another.

Various operating systems differ in the way in which they supply pure standard procedures. In some cases, the procedures are an integral part of the operating system itself; in other systems, they are library programs with the same status as any other program, except that they are marked as pure procedures, and the loader uses this fact to ensure that there is never more than one copy in the store. The advantage of this latter system is that it is much easier to modify existing standard programs or to add new ones.

At the time this is being written, various manufacturers are offering multi-access systems to run on their machines. It is worthy of note that all the more successful systems – as measured by the commercial yardstick of the cost of the services they provide – make heavy use of core swapping and pure procedures. The less successful systems would have little chance of acceptance in the open market; they are used because they are the only ones available on machines which were originally designed and bought for batch processing.

The various systems we have described all offer full multi-access; that is, they permit the user to interact with the monitor, the service programs, and his own program as he pleases.

There is a growing demand for systems which provide conversational access which is cheap but restricted in some way. These systems fall into two groups; those which are dedicated to special systems, and those which offer a full range of facilities, but not all at conversational level.

The first group is typified by those systems which offer a single programming language, together with an editor and a filing system. The user area is kept down to a minimum by keeping each user's program in source form and executing it by interpretation instead of compilation. All the system program is 'pure'; the editor, the interpreter and the basic monitor are very closely linked. These systems are generally available at low cost on small computers, and can only give a restricted service.

The second group of systems, in which the actual conversational access is in some way restricted, seem to offer the best prospects of combining really useful facilities with overall efficiency. Whenever a user is in direct conversational contact with a program of any kind, a part of the cost is that of providing the storage necessary solely for that dialogue. This cost must be paid for either in permanently locked core store or in swapping time.

The amount of storage, and hence this component of the cost, varies according to the type of program with which the user is in contact. It is negligible when talking to the operating system, noticeable for standard programs which are pure procedures, and large for the user's own private programs, or for standard programs which are not re-entrant.

It is evident that if one were to ban or at least discourage certain modes of multi-access, that the cost could be brought down, or the facilities on any given machine could be offered to a larger number of simultaneous users.

This idea leads to the concept of a spectrum in which the variable is the degree of multi-access permitted.

Batch processing	Remote job initiation	Interactive editing	Full multi-access

Direction of increasing
multi-access

The first step towards multi-access is a system with so-called 'remote job initiation'. Basically, this is a batch-processing system with an input well and a filing system, where the normal input and output peripherals are complemented by a set of consoles. To run a job (which could be a compilation followed by an execution, or a call to an off-line editor) the user types the job on the console, and the operating system merely copies it into the input well alongside documents read from other input peripherals. When the job is complete, the system puts it on to a queue and eventually runs it. Finally, the results are taken from the output well and listed on the original console. This system has an efficiency very close to that of a pure batch processing system, but is not conversational in any real sense. However, its turn-round time can be kept down to a few minutes by restricting the sizes of jobs, and by giving higher priority to those entered on consoles. Under these circumstances, it offers definite advantages over the turn-round of several hours which is usual with batch processing systems.

The next step is to permit the users conversational access to certain standard programs. In a context where the chief activity is the development and testing of programs, conversational access can be provided to editors, or compilers, or both. There are real advantages in interactive editors, because they are much quicker and more relaxed to use. On the other hand, conversational compilers (although they have their advocates) seem to offer very little. Although they purport to give an error analysis after every line (so that the line can be repeated if necessary) there are numerous types of errors which cannot be detected until the program is complete. As every programmer knows, the most time-consuming errors are not the syntactic ones which are easily picked up by the compiler, but the more subtle ones which make a program with correct syntax give wrong answers. Conversational compilers do not appear to offer any more assistance in finding such faults than the conventional variety. Furthermore, conversational compilers encourage the composition of programs actually at the console, a practice which is condemned by even the strongest proponents of multi-access.

The principles of partially restricted multi-access have been applied in the outstandingly successful TITAN operating system at Cambridge University. Here, users are allowed to run their jobs in either of two modes: 'expensive' and 'normal'. In the expensive mode, full conversational access to all programs is permitted. In the normal mode, dialogue is permitted only with the operating system itself and with an editor (which is a pure procedure). Any compilation or execution of a compiled program must be initiated through the batch mode. The response of the system is almost instantaneous when editing, but is slightly longer – usually 10–20 seconds – where a compilation has been requested. Since the result of such a compilation is a list of all the syntactic errors in the program (if there are any) users do not feel that the response time is at all slow. Most users are strongly discouraged from using the expensive mode by administrative measures, but it is reported that even those who have a completely free choice continue to use normal mode, saying that for their particular jobs it is not noticeably inferior.

The central processor efficiency which has been achieved with this method is remarkably high. The multi-access system is completely integrated with the batch-processing service run on the same machine, and does not degrade it to any marked degree. The central processor spends 87 per cent of its time doing users' programs, 12 per cent in organisation of the operating system itself, and only 1 per cent idling. These figures should be compared with the central processor efficiencies of 10 to 20 per cent quoted for many other multi-access systems.

14 The Deadly Embrace

A quarrel is quickly settled when deserted by one party; there is no battle unless there be two. Seneca.

Throughout this book, we have referred to the 'deadly embrace' as an eventuality to be avoided at all costs. In this chapter, we consider the conditions under which it can arise, and the methods used to mitigate its effect.

The deadly embrace is a permanent danger in any situation where several processes are competing for the same resources. When a process is initiated, it will already have certain requirements in terms of core store. As it proceeds, it may issue requests to the operating system for further resources, such as more core store, file space, or peripheral devices. Sometimes, the process may release resources as soon as it has finished with them, but often it keeps them until it has ended completely.

In most computing systems, many processes run simultaneously. Sometimes, a resource requested by one process may not be immediately available, and the process is made to wait until the resource is freed. The deadly embrace situation only occurs when two (or more) processes make demands which hold each other up in such a way that neither can proceed. To give a simple illustration, consider a multiprogramming computer with one card reader and one line printer. Suppose that the operating system loads and starts two programs, P_1 and P_2. Immediately on starting, P_1 requests – and receives – the line printer, and P_2 is allocated the card reader. Both programs run. Some time later, P_1 issues a request for the card reader. It is refused, because the card reader is allocated to P_2, so P_1 is suspended. Now, P_2 asks for the line printer. This request is also refused, because the printer belongs to P_1. Both programs are suspended, and neither can start without wrecking the other. The deadly embrace has set in.

In principle, this situation is not limited to two processes, but can involve a ring or chain of processes of any length.

The seriousness of a deadly embrace depends on the type of process which has been stopped. All stoppages are wasteful, since they involve the idleness of those resources which have already been allocated.

Under certain conditions, it is possible to 'borrow' a resource such as a card reader from one process, and to give it back later, but such an action can only be initiated by a human operator, and is extremely prone to errors.

Quite frequently, it is possible to abort one of the processes involved in the deadlock, so that the others can be given the resources they need and can run to completion. The process which was aborted will probably have to be completely restarted, so that all the work carried out up to the time of the deadlock will have been wasted.

Unfortunately, many of the lengthy processes run by a machine in a commercial installation are concerned with altering files or records. If such a process is stopped prematurely, it may well leave the files and their directories in disarray, with only half the amendments made. Any attempt to use such files – even to repeat the process which was stopped – may well end in catastrophic failure, as the file directories, which are usually written last, will not match the actual entries. A deadly embrace between two such processes is truly disastrous.

There are a number of ways in which the risk of a fatal deadlock can be eliminated. In the first place, many of the resources on a machine can be 'stretched' by appropriate software. Thus, a machine with a limited amount of core store can provide a virtual store of almost unlimited size by paging. A system with only one real line printer can effectively offer an arbitrary number of virtual line printers by operating an output well. We shall refer to such resources as 'elastic', and note that if suitable software is indeed provided, we do not need to take these resources into account when considering deadlocks; elastic resources cannot cause them.

The deadly embrace due to non-elastic resources can be avoided by making the processes conform to one of two simple rules:

Either, no process is allowed to start until all the resources it needs are free; then they are all allocated to the process at the same time, and are not used by any other process until this one has finished with them.

Or, all the non-elastic resources are given arbitrary but fixed serial numbers 1, 2, 3 . . . by the designer of the operating system, and each process is only allowed to request resources in strictly ascending order of serial number. Furthermore, it is not permitted to make any request unless the previous one has been satisfied.

The justification for the first rule is self-evident. The effectiveness of the second rule can be proved as follows:

Consider a system with many processes. At any moment, one of them will own a resource with a higher serial number than any owned by another process. This process will be free to run, because the only additional resources it is allowed to ask for must necessarily have even higher serial numbers, and must therefore be free. The system will therefore always contain at least one process which is free to run, although the identity of this process may change from moment to moment. It follows that, if, from any given time, no new processes are initiated, all the processes currently in the system must eventually run to completion; deadlock cannot occur.

These two rules, although both guaranteed to prevent deadlock, can be wasteful by forcing processes to issue requests for resources long before they are needed. The whole subject has received a full theoretical treatment by Habermann, of whose approach we give a short summary.

Habermann's method relies on detecting and avoiding states in which deadlocks may arise. The method depends on advance information about what resources each process will require during its run. This information is clearly vital; without it, no system could guarantee safety, as two processes might simultaneously ask for all the resources in the machine. Fortunately, it is nearly always available, either from job descriptions or from information generated internally by the operating system. The method can be expressed in graph theoretic form. First, we use a tableau in which each column represents a resource, and each row a process. A cell in the tableau contains a 1 if the process in that row uses (or might use) the resource in that column, either directly by requesting an allocation, or indirectly by initiating another process which uses the resource.(Example given on left.)

Second, we have a directed graph. Each node is a process, and a directed arc goes from

Process	Resource				
	A	B	C	D	E
P_1	1	1			
P_2	1	1	1		
P_3		1	1	1	
P_4			1	1	1

node j to node k if process j uses any of the resources which process k will or might use later on. Each possible set of allocations will give rise to a particular graph.

Any individual allocation may result in a new arc or arcs on the graph. For example, if resource C is assigned to P_4, the tableau shows that arcs must be drawn from node 4 to nodes 3 and 2.

In graph theoretic terms, Habermann's rule is that a state is unsafe if its graph contains any closed circuit.

In an operating system which used Habermann's method, every request for the allocation of a resource would be treated as shown in Fig. 14.1.

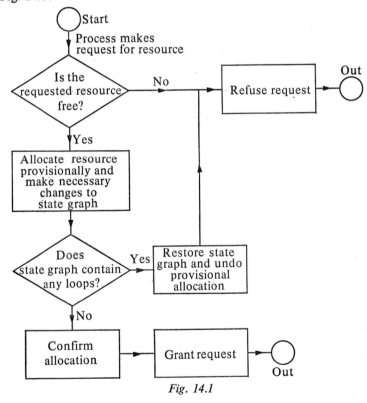

Fig. 14.1

Lastly, we shall give an example. We suppose that the four processes in the tableau above are started simultaneously, and that they make requests in a random order.

101

Event	Effect	Graph
Initially	All four processes free	
P_1 requests A	Granted	
P_2 requests C	Granted	
P_2 requests B	Refused because nodes 1 and 2 would form a loop. P_2 suspended	
P_3 requests B	Refused, because nodes 1,2,3 would form a loop. P_3 suspended	
P_4 requests D.	Granted	
P_1 requests B	Granted	
P_1 ends.	A, B released B assigned to P_2 C_2 freed	
P_2 requests A etc.	Granted etc.	

15 Scheduling

'Then you keep moving round, I suppose?' said Alice.
'Exactly so', said the Hatter: 'as the things get used up'.
'But what happens when you come to the beginning again?' Alice ventured to ask.

Lewis Carroll, *Alice in Wonderland.*

'Scheduling' is the process of deciding the order in which a set of given tasks is to be carried out.

Earlier computers, including those controlled by batch monitors were always fed one job at a time. The order of jobs was decided by the human operator, and there was no need for an automatic scheduling program. Scheduling is inevitably tied up with multi-programming systems, which normally contain several jobs at any one time.

In modern systems, it is almost universal for scheduling to be carried out at three quite different levels. In a batch processing system, there will typically be a number of distinct jobs. Some will have been started, and there will be corresponding processes in the store. Others will still be waiting in the input well for sufficient resources to become free. (At this point, the reader is strongly urged to refer back to Chapters 3 and 4, to refresh his memory about the nature of processes and their control).

The lowest level of scheduling is that of interrupt routines. These are handled in a section of the operating system which is almost separated from the other parts. The actual scheduling of interrupt routines is fairly simple because each routine is of known duration, and the relative priority of the routine is fixed by the designer and expressed by the position of each peripheral device in the interrupt register.

The task of the next level is to decide which *process*, out of those which are elegible to run, is to be started next. This is often called the 'low-level scheduler', and is part of the control mechanism we described in Chapter 4. It is entered whenever a communication extracode has altered the process state tables in any way. Most processes will have repeated contact with the low-level scheduler; every time that a process issues a 'suspend-me' extracode, it is the low level scheduler which eventually restarts that process.

The high-level scheduler is the third and last decision-making component of the system. It is normally entered whenever some resource (like a peripheral device or an area of store) has been released, and it determines whether a new job can be started. It takes its decision according to such criteria as which resources are free, which job in the queue has the highest priority, and which one has been waiting longest.

On a multi-access system, the high-level scheduler has a relatively trivial task; it must allow all jobs presented on consoles to start unless the system is so full as to be incapable of accepting any more.

There is a correspondence between the activities of the two schedulers and a subdivision of basic resources into 'elastic' and 'nonelastic', as described in Chapter 14.

The connection between this concept and that of scheduling is that low-level schedulers are only used to reallocate elastic resources, the allocation of the inelastic ones being left to the high-level scheduler.

To understand the functioning of the low-level scheduler, let us consider the process tables described in Chapter 4. We shall suppose that the tables only contain processes which can be effected by the central processor; this is legitimate because we can assume that peripheral processes are now handled by interrupt routines. Each record in the tables refers to a process which may either be free to run, or suspended for some reason connected with a semaphore. The format of the record is bound to vary from system to system, but it must contain, or at least point to, a block of data which is sufficient to restart the process by resetting the datum-limit or page address registers in the right way and then transferring control to the right instruction. The record may also include other fields which contain the 'reason for suspension', and links for the various chains of which it is part.

The main object of the low-level scheduler must be to ensure that all the parts of the machine are fully utilised. In the multi-access mode, it has the important ancillary job of seeing that all jobs are moved forward at an even rate, and that no one job is held up at the expense of another.

In a batch-processing environment, one way of achieving these aims is to give each process a numerical 'priority'. The highest priority is assigned to those processes which drive the fastest peripheral devices and the lowest is given to those which rely completely on the central processor.

The low level scheduler always selects and runs the free process with the highest priority. In a multi-processor system, a process which is actually being run by one processor is regarded as not 'eligible for running' by the others.

To organise this system, the process records can be chained together, as shown in Fig. 15.1. (This drawing is simplified and does not show the 'state vector' field in each record.) It also omits the fact that the various chains may be linked in both directions.

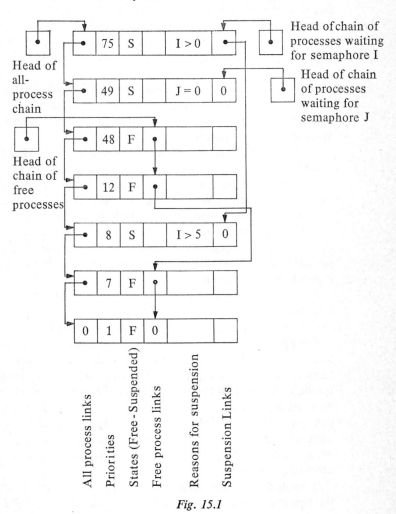

Fig. 15.1

In the main chain, all the process records are arranged in order of decreasing priority. There is also a sub-chain of the records of free processes, and a sub-chain of records of processes for each semaphore which is currently causing suspension. Whenever the status of a record is changed, it is moved from one chain to another. The correct place of insertion can usually be determined by passing over a very small number of links, and the next process to be run can be found immediately from the head of the 'free process' chain. The priorities of the various processes are assigned by the operating system, with 'private' processes (such as input or output well servicing) always having higher priorities than those which belong to users' programs. Many systems have a periodic 'review' of priorities, so that if, for example, the job with lowest priority has not been advanced at all throughout a given review period, it has its priority increased. This prevents compute-bound jobs from using up large areas of core store ineffectively for long periods.

Another method of running the low-level scheduler is not to use priorities but to arrange the various free process records into a ring. Every time that the low-level scheduler is called, it advances one step round the ring. Whenever a process previously suspended is freed, it is added to the ring. Processes which 'belong' to the operating system are inserted immediately ahead of the current process, so that they are started quickly; but processes which belong to a user are generally placed behind the current one, so that a full cycle has to elapse before they are reached.

This system automatically implements the 'round robin' principle, and this makes it suitable for multi-access.

In many multi-access systems (and in some batch processors) the restarting of a process may involve some preliminary core swapping. Needless to say, it is not part of the scheduler's duty to organise this transfer by itself, holding everything up, until it is completed. If the scheduler detects that the next process to be started is not present in the core, then it will initiate a special process to fetch it into the core, and arrange for a special semaphore to suspend the 'selected' process until it is ready. The 'fetching' process itself is likely to initiate other processes for finding space in the core, for selecting a process to swap out, and so on.

We now come to the subject of high-level scheduling. This part of the operating system is important if all or even part of the load is carried out under batch processing conditions; for instance, it forms a vital component of the TITAN restricted multi-access system at Cambridge.

The high-level scheduler is called whenever some major resource is freed. It searches through the input well, and maintains a list of jobs which are complete and ready to be started. It decides which jobs (if any) are to be transferred from the waiting list to the 'active' status. Once a job is chosen, a 'job control' process is activated and begins to execute the primitive operations specified for that job.

The design of high-level schedulers is particularly difficult because it is never clear exactly what is to be optimised. Every system has to handle a certain proportion of 'awkward' jobs which have to be run in a way which forces inefficient operation. If a high-level scheduler aims solely at maximising the use of all components of the machine, the awkward jobs are likely to be held up indefinitely. If, on the other hand, one follows a 'first in – first out' policy, then many small jobs may be held up behind one large one, and cause distress to a large number of users. In practice, the scheduling policy has to be a compromise in which several conflicting factors are taken into account. The policy is often expressed in a formula which includes various coefficients which are meant to represent the cost of forcing customers to wait, and to measure their annoyance. Since these quantities – even if they exist – are impossible to measure, coefficients in the formula cannot be 'tuned' to optimise anything, and the manager has to rely on his own common sense. It is thus very hard to say which of two scheduling algorithms is the better.

Many jobs make use of specially prepared devices, like tape decks loaded with specified tapes, or line printers fitted with pre-printed stationery. It is obviously advantageous for the operators to be given advance warning of such requirements, so that they can set up the devices *before* they are actually required. In many systems the high-level scheduler is responsible for this kind of advance planning as well, using information from the job description.

We shall illustrate the ideas involved in high-level scheduling by describing the techniques used in two typical systems.

The JUNE system, in use at Lancaster University, is simpler than most because it is designed specifically for a small machine and can only run jobs one at a time. All jobs are assumed to need the line printer, and input is taken from a well, so that the only variable resources are the magnetic tape decks. The only way in which the scheduler can affect the efficiency of use of the machine is to give plenty of advance warning for magnetic tape requirements; otherwise, it concentrates on maximising 'user satisfaction'.

Whenever it is called (usually just after a job has ended), the high-level scheduler goes through the input well and calculates a 'priority' for each job waiting there. (This priority has nothing to do with the priority of *processes* mentioned earlier in this chapter.) The priority formula is chosen so as to favour short jobs with small amounts of output, and jobs which have been waiting a long time; it is

$$P = AGE^2 - SECONDS \text{ (OF MILL TIME)} - 16* OUTPUT \text{ (LINES)}$$

where two of the quantities are estimates taken from the job description, and one is the time which the job has been waiting in the input well, in minutes.

It then goes through the jobs again and picks out those which involve the use of magnetic tape (JUNE job descriptions include the identities of any tapes needed). For each such job it matches the names of tapes needed with those already mounted, and calculates a 'tape loading cost' which is 2^{13} units for each tape that has to be loaded, and 2^{12} for each one which has to be unloaded. It then chooses the tape job for which the expression (Priority – tape loading cost) has the highest value, and instructs the operator to make the necessary tape changes. It also sets up a 'booking' for that job, allowing 1 minute for each tape to be loaded, and 30 seconds for each one to be unloaded. This whole step is omitted if there is already a booking in force.

Finally, the system scans the entire job list again and actually starts the job with the highest priority. For this purpose a large number (100000) is added if a job is the subject of a booking which has 'matured' (so that the necessary tapes can be presumed to be mounted), or subtracted if the job has had a booking made so recently that the tapes cannot yet be ready.

The general pattern presented by this system is that tape jobs alternate with groups of small non-tape jobs. The instructions for mounting a new set of tapes usually appear immediately after each tape job has finished, and the operator can mount them while the system is doing other work. The system tends to do short jobs very quickly, but occasionally it will do a long job which has been in the input well so long that its AGE^2 term outweighs the others. This pattern will only emerge if the system is fed with a well spread 'mix' of jobs. If it is fed only with tape jobs, the 'advance warning' system cannot function correctly.

The scheduler on the ATLAS 1 computer is more complicated. When jobs appear in the input well, they are sorted into three different queues: 'short' jobs, which specify less than a certain amount of mill time and have no special peripheral requirements; 'tape' jobs, which use one or more private magnetic tapes; and 'long jobs' which are dominated by the mill time they need. The system attempts to keep one job out of each category in the active state, so as to keep the various parts of the machine fully occupied. The jobs in each queue are run in sequence, unless one should happen to be marked as a high priority job, in which case it is allowed to join the head of the queue. Whenever a tape job is started, instructions are immediately issued for loading the tapes needed by the next one in the queue. This is possible because most ATLAS installations have enough tape decks to have several spare at any one time.

This system has to have special facilities for handling jobs which take up all the resources; but calls on these facilities are kept down by informing the users that they must not exceed certain limits of store or numbers of tape decks without prior permission from the computer manager.

16 Accounting and Control

This chapter is concerned with the management of large computers. In the first few years of computing, a machine in any organisation was usually accessible on a 'free for all' basis (in both senses). No attempt was made to monitor the amount of time used for any project or to exercise any control over the quality of programming.

Recently, computing has come to be used on so wide a scale that it is necessary to employ management techniques. The activities of the computer manager may sometimes appear irksome to individual users, but they are essential to the provision of the computing service as a whole.

Management is not necessary for small machines and those being used for special purposes (like theatre booking). It becomes important only when a system carries numerous users each working on independent projects. Machines used in this way are found in two environments; in commercial service bureaux, and as 'in-house' machines in organisations like universities, government departments and large industrial firms.

The management problem is relatively easier to solve in bureaux, because the manager is not concerned with optimising the use of the computer. He is only interested in selling as much computer time as possible, and in ensuring that legitimate users receive accounts at periodic intervals.

When the machine is used on an 'in-house' basis, the problems of management are far more difficult. The computer manager is usually assigned fixed resources in terms of a given computer and a specific budget to cover all the maintenance, staff and stationery costs. He is expected to supply a demand from within the organisation that is nearly always greater than his resources can stand. Furthermore, his chances of obtaining extra resources on a short-term time scale are normally non-existent. Under these circumstances, it is very import-ant for the machine to be used as efficiently as possible, so that it will process the largest amount of work.

Modern general-purpose machines normally handle so much work that accounting and control procedures must be automated. It is usual for these procedures to be made part of the operating system, but it is impossible to put them together in one 'package'; rather, they must be distributed to key points, like the interrupt routines controlling peripherals, where they test, measure and record every-thing which the system does on behalf of any job.

A job's first encounter with a control procedure is the routine check applied to see whether the user is authorised. As we explained in a previous chapter, this is done with the aid of a list of names or 'project numbers', and possibly a set of secret passwords.

In a bureau environment, the only other important task of the accounting section is to keep records which can be used to generate regular invoices for the customers. The usual method of charging is to put a flat rate on each of the various resources offered. A typical price list for a batch-processing system might be:

Central processor time	£0.05 per second
Store	£0.08 per block per minute
Output (line printer)	£0.05 per page
Input (cards)	£0.25 per 100 cards
File space	£0.50 per block per month
Hire of magnetic tape	£1.00 per month
Charge for mounting a tape	£0.50 (each)

In a multi-access system, one could have the additional item:

Connect time	£2.00 per hour (this is the time for which a console is actually on-line).

It is usual to charge small customers a fee calculated directly on these rates, although sometimes a minimum periodic charge is speci-fied. Larger customers, and those who are willing to use the system at unpopular times may get rebates.

To automate charging, operating systems usually contain an 'accounts file' as part of their filing systems. This may be divided into documents, one for each user. During each job, the use of each re-source is constantly measured, and, when the job ends, a record is

111

appended to the appropriate document. Further necessary information, such as the amount of file space used by each customer and the number of magnetic tapes assigned to him, is also recorded daily. At intervals, this information is used to produce bills.

In the situation where the machine is used only by members of one organisation, and the total resources are fixed, the main object of the accounting and control system must be to encourage efficient use of the computer. It is important that the operating system should do so according to the policies decided by the computer manager, and not on its own inflexible lines.

The methods available for controlling the use of a computer (in the absence of genuine charging) are:

(1) *Rationing* Each user is given a budget of resources which has to last him a certain time. He understands that if he should run out of resources prematurely, then he will find it very difficult to get more.

(2) *Control of access* As a general rule, it can be said that experienced users write better, more efficient programs than novices. It is possible to restrict the use of the various facilities to those who have proved their competence in the appropriate field.

(3) *Continuous monitoring* It is nearly always the case that a few very large regular jobs account for a substantial portion of the total resources of any installation. It is always worth while to examine these jobs very carefully to ensure that the problem analysis and programming have been properly carried out. It is quite common for the efficiency of a program to be doubled by writing one inner loop in machine code, and to be improved by a factor of 10 by the use of a better numerical method.

The application of all three methods of control can be greatly assisted by special procedures in the operating system.

In budgetary systems, it is common for each entry in the list of authorised users to contain two figures – the total allowance for the current period, and the amount of resources used so far. The figures are usually expressed in money, and sometimes in 'computer time', (an almost meaningless concept in this context). Whenever a user submits a job, the budget is checked, and the job is rejected if the remaining allowance is negative. In a batch-processing system, where an estimate of the total resource requirements must be given, the job may be rejected if the remaining allowance is insufficient to run it, even though it may still be positive. Some systems are a little more lenient; for example, the JUNE system only rejects a job when the estimate is more than twice the remaining budget. In no system is a job, once accepted, ever stopped because its periodic allowance (as opposed to its individual resource estimate) has run out.

In GEORGE 3, where the file store has a hierarchical structure, the budgets are also assigned hierarchically. Each user receives his allowance from his superior, and is free to assign it to those responsible to him in any way he pleases. Whenever a resource is actually used, it is subtracted from each of the whole chain of budgets up to the highest level.

Sometimes, the system controls the actual number of jobs put through the machine by each user in any one day or week. This discourages the tendency of many amateur programmers to make repeated compilations and tests of the same program without really searching for all the errors. It also prevents the very common abuse which consists of splitting one large job into several small ones, so as to get them through the system at a time when there is a limit in force on individual job size.

Control of access can be achieved by a mechanism of the same type as budgetary control. Each user is given a 'permission vector' which consists of Boolean elements. Each element refers to one of the facilities offered by the system, and has the value 'true' if the user is licensed to use that facility. In the JUNE system, there is a permission bit for each language, and separate elements to give or withold the right to use magnetic tape, multi-access, or more than set minima of core store and mill time per job.

When a new user applies for facilities on the machine, he is obliged to present evidence of competence in the language he intends to use, unless it is a standard package with simple rules for data preparation. His permission vector is constructed and entered into the user file accordingly.

Lastly, the operating system can help in the task of continuous monitoring by indicating who are the heavy users of the machine.

In the form they stand, these methods of control have several deficiencies. There is no way of giving important users priority over others. There is no way of spreading demand evenly over the twenty-four hours, and it is likely that the system's performance will be degraded during the day by an excessively large number of users, but that at night the machine will be under-used. Lastly, the control

113

methods permit the unfortunate state of affairs where a user is barred from a machine which is idle because his allowance has run out.

The solution adopted to this problem in the TITAN operating system at Cambridge is to divide the day into three shifts, and each shift into four priorities. Each user is given 12 allowances, one for each shift and priority. Some of the allowances may be zero, but at the lowest priority, the allowances are effectively infinite. The assignment of budgets depends partly on the user's need, and partly on what resources remain available. Classes and demonstrations take precedence during the day, so that many users have to be content with the evening or night-time for much of their allowances. Most users are given 'ordinary' priority, and the 'high' and 'top' priority categories are quite rarely used.

When the machine is running, jobs of higher priority are always given precedence over those of lower priority. This means that if the machine is idle, anyone can use it, even though his 'ordinary' allowance has run out.

One very important aspect of accounting is the correct choice of units. This point is well illustrated by the method used at Cambridge (and since copied at Lancaster University) for controlling the use of file space. The obvious, but wrong unit of accounting would have been the block, containing a fixed number of characters. In a naive system, each user would be assigned so many blocks of file store and would be constrained to keep all his documents within that space. He would never be allowed to use more blocks, and would have no incentive to use less. This would result in a wasteful use of space, because the file store would be cluttered up with numerous documents which were not in frequent use, but which occupied space that kept other, more deserving documents out.

The Cambridge system is based on the observation that people tend to write, test and run programs in bursts of activity lasting a few days, after which the programs may remain unused for long periods. In this system, the unit is the 'block-day'. Each user has a regular income of block-days, and a 'current balance'. Every day the balance is augmented by the income, and diminished by the number of blocks he occupies at that moment. If his occupancy is less than his income, his balance will gradually increase; on the other hand, if he is using more blocks than his income, his balance will drop until it is negative. A user with a negative balance is subject to certain sanctions; for example, he may not create any new documents. As his balance grows more and more negative, so the punishments applied by the system grow more severe. In the extreme, after many warnings, the user may find that all his documents have been dumped on magnetic tape and erased from the random access file store.

The system is designed to encourage thrift and planning in the use of file storage. A user who is currently inactive can withdraw all his documents from the file store by ordering them to be relegated to a magnetic tape. Since he now occupies only a small number of blocks, his balance can grow to a figure which is many times his daily income. When the time comes to develop a new program, he can use up all his savings in a burst of timely extravagance – for a few days, he can have all the file space he wants.

The system is open to the theoretical objection that all the users may decide to cash their saved-up space at the same time, and that this will overtax the capacity of the disk file. In practice, this is very unlikely to happen.

A good analogy can be drawn with a bank; most branches only carry enough cash to supply their daily needs, and would be unable to pay out if all the depositors were to ask for their money at the same time. Nevertheless, this does not seem to worry the bank's clients unduly. Banks can always pay unless they are already suspect and there is a run on them.

References

Atkinson, M. P., Lister, A. M., and Colin, A. J. T., 'Multi-access facilities in a single stream batch processing system', *The Computer Bulletin*, Vol. 14, No. 3 (March 1970), pp. 75–77.

Barron, D. W., *Assemblers and Loaders* (MacDonald/American Elsevier Computer Monographs – 1969).

Barron, D. W., Fraser, A. G., Hartley, D. F., Landy, B., and Needham, R. M., 'File handling at Cambridge University', *AFIPS Spring Joint Computer Conference*, Vol. 30 (April 1967), pp. 163–167.

Coffman, E. G., Elphick, M. J., and Shoshani, A., 'System Deadlocks', *A.C.M. Computer Surveys,* Vol. 3, No. 2 (June 1971), pp. 67–78.

Colin, A. J. T., 'The Lancaster University Operating System', *The Computer Bulletin*, Vol. 12, No. 7 (Nov. 1968), pp. 247–255.

Colin, A. J. T., 'DOLPHIN – A text filing system for University use', *The Computer Journal*, Vol. 13, No. 2 (May 1970), pp. 136–141.

Cuttle, G., and Robinson, P. B., (Ed), *Executive Programs and Operating Systems* (MacDonald/American Elsevier Computer Monographs – 1970).

Daley, R. C., and Dennis, J. B., 'Virtual Memory, Processes, and Sharing in MULTICS', *Comm. A.C.M.*, Vol. 11, No. 5 (May 1968), pp. 306–312.

Dijkstra, E. W., 'The Structure of the "THE" – Multiprogramming System', *Comm. A.C.M.*, Vol. 11, No. 5 (May 1968), pp. 341–346.

Foster, J. M., *List Processing* (MacDonald/American Elsevier Computer Monographs 1967).

Fraser, A. G., 'User Control in a multi-access system,' *The Computer Journal*, Vol. 11, No. 1 (May 1968), pp. 12–16.

Fraser, A. G., 'Integrity of a mass storage filing system', *The Computer Journal*, Vol. 12, No. 1 (Feb. 1969), pp. 1–5.

116

Gill, S., and Samet, P. A., 'Charging for computer time in universities', *The Computer Bulletin*, Vol. 13, No. 1 (Jan. 1969), pp. 14–16.

Habermann, A. N., 'Prevention of System Deadlocks', *Comm. A.C.M.*, Vol. 12, No. 7 (July 1969), pp. 373–377 and 385.

Hartley, D. F., Landy, B., and Needham, R. M., 'The structure of a multiprogramming supervisor', *The Computer Journal*, Vol. 11, No. 3 (Nov. 1968), pp. 247–255.

Hartley, D. F., (Ed) *The Cambridge Multiple-Access System, User's Reference Manual* (University Mathematical Laboratory, Cambridge – 1968).

Hartley, D. F., 'Management Software in Multiple-Access Systems', *Bulletin of I.M.A.*, Vol. 6, No. 1 (April 1970), pp. 11–13.

Howarth, D. J., Jones, P. D., and Wyld, M. T., 'The Atlas scheduling system', *The Computer Journal*, Vol. 5, No. 3 (Oct. 1962), pp. 238–244.

Howarth, D. J., Payne, R. B., and Sumner, F. H., 'The Manchester University Atlas Operating System Part II: Users' Description', *The Computer Journal*, Vol. 4, No. 3 (Oct. 1961), pp. 226–229.

I.B.M. System 360/Operating System Concepts and Facilities (*C28–6535*) (I.B.M. Corp.)

Kilburn, T., Payne, R. B., and Howarth, D. J., 'The Atlas Supervisor', *Proc. E.J.C.C.* (Dec. 1961).

Kilburn, T., Howarth, D. J., Payne, R. B., and Sumner, F. H., 'The Manchester University Atlas Operating System Part I: Internal Organisation', *The Computer Journal*, Vol. 4, No. 3 (Oct. 1961), pp. 222–225.

Knuth, D. E., *The Art of Computer Programming*, Vol. 1/Fundamental Algorithms (Addison-Wesley Publishing Co. – 1968).

Oestreicher, M. D., Bailey, M. J., Strauss, J. I. 'GEORGE 3 – 'A General Purpose Time Sharing and Operating System', *Comm. A.C.M.*, Vol. 10, No. 11 (Nov. 1967), pp. 685–693.

Operating Systems George 1 and 2 (4229) (I.C.L. – 1970).

Operating Systems George 3 and 4 (4169) (I.C.L. – 1969).

Ore, O., *Graphs and Their Uses* (Random House, New Mathematical Library, Vol. 10 – 1963).

PDP-10 Reference Handbook (Digital Equipment Corp. – 1970).

PLAN Reference Manual (4004) (I.C.L. – 1967).

REFERENCES

Randell, B., and Kuehner, C. J., 'Dynamic Storage Allocation Systems', *Comm. A.C.M.*, Vol. 11, No. 5 (May 1968), pp. 297–306.

Samet, P. A., 'Measuring the efficiency of software', *The Computer Bulletin*, Vol. 13, No. 10 (Oct. 1969), pp. 351–352.

Sayre, D., 'Is Automatic "Folding" of Programs Efficient Enough to Displace Manual?', *Comm. A.C.M.*, Vol. 12, No. 12 (Dec. 1969), pp. 656–660.

Wilkes, M. V., *'Time-sharing Computer Systems'* (MacDonald/American Elsevier Computer Monographs 1968).

Index

119